The World of
POLO
Past & Present

BY THE SAME AUTHOR

The World of POLO *Past & Present*

J. N. P. WATSON

Foreword by The Viscount Cowdray

Salem House
Topsfield, Massachusetts

© J. N. P. Watson 1986

First published in the United States
by Salem House Publishers, 1986
462 Boston Street
Topsfield, Massachusetts 01983

ISBN 0–88162–203–6

Library of Congress Catalog Card
Number 86–60541

CONTENTS

FOREWORD

BY THE VISCOUNT COWDRAY T.D.

Chairman of the Hurlingham Polo Association, 1947–1967

I am very happy to write a foreword to John Watson's book which to the best of my knowledge is the first condensed history of this ancient and fascinating game, still the fastest ever invented. He has put an immense amount of research and hard work into what must have been a labour of love. While it is not possible, in the scope of one volume to give a full picture of polo in the many countries across the globe where it is played, this book can fairly claim to prove the first comprehensive account of the development of the game and its place in the world now.

As John Watson's writing shows the story of polo must be one of the most romantic of all sporting sagas. Starting at the Imperial Court of ancient Persia it was taken up by the Moguls of Hindustan, the Chinese, Tibetans and Japanese. In the middle of the 19th century tea-planters and army officers emulated the native players of Manipur; while, quite separately, in 1869, a group of cavalrymen stationed in the South of England developed their own brand of polo after reading reports of the Asian game. Gaining quick and widespread popularity English polo was soon identified with the shining names of Hurlingham, Ranelagh and Roehampton.

The proprietor of the *New York Times* took the English concept of polo to the United States in 1876 and, from that introduction, the famous Anglo-American Westchester Cup series – a full record of which is given here – began ten years later. As the author points out, the 'twenties and 'thirties were the "Golden Age" of American polo when the American Open was what the Argentine Open is today; and for the Americans probably the great landmark was the hard-fought East-West series of the 'thirties, when the West first challenged successfully the supremacy of the East.

Meanwhile the English speaking ranchers in the Argentine started playing on their estancias thus launching that country on a career that would lead them to the forefront of the game internationally. By the end of the 19th century the British, mainly through the Royal Navy, had introduced their game to a host of other countries, too.

The author, a former player, who has been well known over many years for his regular reports of the tournaments in *Country Life* and *The Times*, provides a general review of the rise of the game in the United States, South America, Australia, New Zealand and other countries where polo flourishes. He starts his book with a lucid ABC of the rudiments of the game and ends with an informative survey of the character and image of polo today and its place in the modern sporting world.

◁ *Foreword* ▷

Polo is growing fast in popularity and this book with its wonderful collection of prose and poetry quotations provides a unique background, all under one cover, for everyone who is involved, and will add to the interest of players and spectators in the game. For instance the abolition of the off-side rule forced an absolute revolution in tactics, since when tactics have not altered basically. Positional play and cross-passing, continuous interchange at full gallop, or a combination of both? Tactical theories are continually confounded by exceptions that prove the rule and on top of it all depend on the horses available of which no two are alike. The abolition of the height limit demanded better horsemanship.

Having been closely involved in international polo since the 1930s and having played a leading role in the resurrection of the game in post-war England I am delighted that all the polo aspirations, managerial efforts, pony-breeding achievements, gamesmanship and athleticism of the past century and more are placed on record in this fine book.

Cowdray

JANUARY, 1986

PREFACE

This is not intended to be a comprehensive world history of polo, but rather a survey of the game's origin in the ancient East, and its emergence in India under the British *Raj*; subsequently, its mainstream development through the England of the 1870s to the United States of the 1880s; so to South America where the game would one day reach its gladiatorial peak; and – mostly via British India and the Royal Navy – to Australia and New Zealand and the nations of Europe, the Middle and Far East and Africa. My modern polo theme therefore concentrates mainly on those countries that have been the principal contenders for world supremacy, and thus on the game's monumental championships – the Westchester Cup, the Cup of the Americas and the Olympic duels – and arenas such as Hurlingham, Meadow Brook and the grounds of Buenos Aires.

To obtain the flavours of the history of any sport a strongly representative array of illustrations is, I believe, an indispensable adjunct to the narrative. I hope that the collection assembled here tells the reader at least as much as the text does about the image and romance of polo over the past century and more.

I would like to place on record the warm thanks I owe to the many people who have helped to bring *The World of Polo* to fruition. To Major William Loyd, who was manager of the Guards Polo Club from 1973 to 1985. Apart from reading my typescripts and making many useful suggestions he put me in touch with several authorities overseas and lent me a number of interesting books on the subject. To Mr Summerfield K. Johnston Jr, chairman of the United States Polo Association, Mr William T. Ylvisaker, founder of both the West Palm Beach Polo and Country Club and the American Polo Foundation, and Mr Philip Iglehart for giving up their time, during my 1985 visit to Florida, to provide me with information on the American polo scene: and to the Anglo-Argentine player, Mr Robert Graham, who lent me books and periodicals on polo in the Argentine and patiently instructed me on the game's situation in that country today.

I am deeply indebted to Lt-Col. Alec Harper, the Hurlingham Polo Association's honorary secretary and a former international player, for casting a careful and critical eye over the last two chapters of the book, for talking to me about the heyday of Indian polo and for giving me access to the HPA's invaluable archives and library in the grounds of his home near Midhurst, Sussex. Also to his assistant, Mrs Judy Duke-

◁ *Preface* ▷

Woolley, who is in charge of the day-to-day running of that office, and who was most cooperative throughout my research.

My thanks are due, too, to Mrs Jeanne Chisholm, of the Chisholm Gallery, Palm Beach, Florida, for her generosity in providing me with colour transparencies of her pictures by G. D. Rowlandson, H. Lucas-Lucas, R. E. Galindo, Cuthbert Bradley, G. D. Armour, "Snaffles", Gilbert Holiday, H. F. Bauer, Neil Cawthorne and Heather St Clair Davis, and also for the loan of a number of photographs. To Miss Brenda de Suze, also of the United States, for our long chat about her travels around the world's polo clubs. To Mr David Walton Masters for providing me a host of colour transparencies from his splendid collection of polo pictures. To the Marques Cassar de Sain and the Marsa Polo Club of Malta for the photographs from that club's albums. And to Mr Miles S. Carpenter for the loan of several photographs.

To Viscount Cowdray for explaining his part in the revival of polo in post-war England and for placing his scrapbooks at my disposal. To the Marquess of Cholmondeley for allowing me to reproduce photographs from his father's regimental and polo albums; and to Mrs Ione O'Brien, for lending me photographs of South American teams that have stayed at her famous polo players' hotel, Park House, Sussex.

To the Editor of *The Times* for permitting me to quote from a journalist's report from Nigeria in February, 1982, from Tim Heald's piece in July, 1984, and my own polo biography of Claire Tomlinson. To Mr Herbert Spencer for allowing me to quote from his *Chakkar*. To Jonathan Cape Ltd and the author for permitting the use of the excerpt from Mr Charles Chenevix Trench's book, *The Frontier Scouts*. To Mrs Gerald Critchley for allowing her delightful poem, *Polo Wives*, to be quoted. To the Sir Alfred Munnings Art Museum for authority to show Munnings's portrait of Devereux Milburn; to Mr Lindsay, Mr Kenneth and Miss Marjorie Edwards for their consent to the use of the illustrations by their father, Lionel Edwards, from *The Maltese Cat*; to Mr Marshall Haseltine for allowing me to reproduce that great bronze *The Big Four*, by his father, Herbert Haseltine; to the Hurlingham Club for allowing me to reproduce *Pavilion 1890* by Jamyn Brooks; to Mr Terence Cuneo for his *Pony Lines, Cirencester, 1972*; Miss Susie Whitcomb for *Coronation Cup, 1979*, and Miss Joan Wanklyn for *Smith's Lawn, 1967*; to *Punch* for granting permission for G. D. Armour's paintings and cartoons to be reproduced; to Mr Edward Horswell, of the Sladmore Gallery, for his advice and help; to the William Marler Gallery, of Cirencester and London, for Gilbert Holiday's *Hurlingham*. And to Messrs Gordon Carlisle, Michael Chevis, Stanley Hurwitz, David Lominska, Mike Roberts, Charles White, the Topham Picture Library and the Hulton Picture Library for their excellent photographs.

To Mrs Audrey Guy who typed the text (as promptly and meticulously as ever); and, most of all to my wife, Lavinia, who typed all the copious correspondence connected with the book and supported me in innumerable other ways, too.

J.N.P.W.

The World of
POLO
Past & Present

Chapter 1

THE GAME

Chukka by chukka the game is played,
So goal by goal point by point is made,
I hope I am never too old and staid
To play the game of Polo.

Think of the pony who turns on his hocks,
As a stream fast flowing, slips round the rocks:
Doesn't that make you rejoice old crocks?
Who once played the game of Polo?

Just think of that darlin' little brown mare
A mouth like silk, you could turn with a hair,
Nor can any possible game compare
With the wonderful game of Polo?

As the years slip by one reminisces,
(One does about games as well as kisses)
I'm inclined to think my greatest bliss is
A real fast game of Polo.

Do they play this game on Olympian Plains?
I will keep my escutcheon free from stains
Or at least I will take the greatest pains
To be fit for Olympian Polo.

H. St C. S. 1922

Polo is the fastest team contest in the world. Fundamentally, it consists of driving a ball three and a half inches in diameter with a long and strangely balanced bamboo mallet from the back of a galloping horse. Your opponents, meanwhile, are constantly trying to obstruct your endeavours in the hope of keeping the ball to themselves. The result is that the play twists and turns relentlessly in a dizzying flurry of sticks and a stampede of ponies' feet. Is it any wonder then that this is a most difficult game to master?

TEAMS LINED UP FOR THE THROW-IN AT THE START OF A MATCH AT HAM. "The Numbers One, Two, Three and Back form up alongside their respective opponents"

Certainly there is more for the beginner to think about – controlling his pony, marking his opposite number, striking and passing the ball, preventing others from hitting the ball, backing up his team-mates, anticipating the tactics and observing the very stringent rules of the game – than in any other comparable sport. It is, moreover, a duel fought with speed and precision, a contest which demands of its players exceptional dash, courage, style, stamina, acrobatic horsemanship and a cooperation so close it is almost telepathic. When played by the high-scoring stars of the game, polo is certainly one of the most breathtaking of all spectator sports.

What is more, it is a sport which is growing in popularity with spectators and participants alike. For this reason, the next few pages have been devoted to an explanation of how the game is played – and what sort of a person you need to be to make a good polo player.

Conditions, Regulations, Positions

The polo pitch is 300 yards long and 200 yards wide. There are white lines at the centre of the ground and penalty lines 30, 40 and 60 yards from each back line. The goal-posts are 10 feet high, standing eight yards apart at the centre of each back line. Some grounds are boarded at the sides to keep the ball more frequently in play. A boarded ground can be narrower.

The winning side is that which scores most goals, that is to say the team that succeeds, according to the rules, in striking the ball most often between their opponents' goal-posts. The game, being divided into four, five or six 7½-minute chukkas, or periods, lasts for a little under, or a little over, the hour. Because polo is played at a more or less continuous gallop, interspaced with sharp, often excruciating stops, twists and turns, it is extremely exacting and tiring even for the fittest ponies. They are therefore exchanged after each chukka, and, as a general rule, no pony is employed for more than two chukkas in any one match. If a match ends in a draw an additional chukka is played and, if no deciding goal is then scored, the players change

2

ponies and ride on for yet another chukka this time with widened goal-posts. (This last applies only under Hurlingham rules.)

The players are numbered One and Two (forwards), Three and Back. The duties of Number One are: in defence, to ride off the opposing Back and prevent him from having an uninterrupted hit at the ball; and, in attack, to give him the slip and wait a pass, or to ride him away from his goal mouth and so leave it open for the Number Two to score. The Number Two is usually the stronger of the two forwards and *should* be the driving force of an attack and the principal goal-scorer. Number Three, the pivot of the team, is usually their best player, so this is the most suitable place for the team captain to play. He will often initiate attacks, and his two first objectives will be to send the ball up to the forwards and to intercept attacks. As principal defender, the Back must be thoroughly reliable. He must be a safe hitter, especially with backhanders. His aim will be to pass the ball to his Number Two; he will mark the opposing Number One. The opposing Number Two and Three also mark each other. But the positions are not rigid and the essence of good polo is in flexibility of teamwork, changing positions as the game dictates.

At the start of the game, the two teams line up in the middle of the ground, each team being on its own side of the halfway line. Numbers One, Two, Three and Back stand alongside their respective opponents. An umpire (there will invariably be two in a match) then bowls the ball underhand between the opposing sides, and the game begins. A goal is scored when the ball (having been hit without incurring an infringement) passes between the posts and over the goal-line. Teams change ends after each goal. Whenever the ball goes over the sideline an umpire throws in a fresh one between the lined-up teams. When it is knocked over the back line, it is then formally hit in by the defenders. If, on the other hand, the ball is knocked over the back line by one of the defenders, the attackers are given a free hit at goal, 60 yards in from the point where it crossed the line.

Fouls and penalties

A tiresome feature of polo from the spectator's point of view, even in matches of the highest class, can be the frequent interruption of play by the umpires owing to fouls. There is no offside rule; players may impede their opponents by knocking and hooking their sticks; they may also lean into them and "ride them off". In fact they will endeavour to do so at every constructive opportunity. But, owing to the inevitable hazards of this fast-moving stick-and-ball mounted duel, certain rules have to be severely enforced. The penalties for riding across another player's "right of way", misuse of the stick, bumping and zigzagging, are instantaneous and severe, taking the form of a 60-, 30- or 40-yard free hit at the offender's goal, or a free shot from the place of the foul. The "right of way" exists during every moment of the game and is owned, in general, by that player who is riding most closely in the direction in which the ball was last hit. It is an offence for another player to cross this line, if, by doing so, there is any possibility of another horse having to check in order to avoid collision. The whole conduct of the game depends upon the right of way. Another infringement is the "foul hook", that is to say any attempt to interfere with an opponent's stick other than when he is in the act of striking a ball. A player may not attempt to hook either across his opponent's pony or when his opponent's stick is above shoulder level. Nor may he "intimidate" an opponent.

"SOME GROUNDS ARE BOARDED." Gonzalo Pieres (handicap 9) of Argentina, in action on the boards during the 1985 World Cup at Palm Beach, Florida. He is 10 in the United States. Handicaps vary according to the ratings awarded by the different national associations (*left*)

"THE BACK MUST BE A SAFE HITTER, ESPECIALLY WITH HIS BACKHANDERS." HRH The Prince of Wales and John Kidd (*right*)

Penalties are referred to by numbers. In the case of penalty No. 1 a goal is given for a dangerous or deliberate foul in the vicinity of the goal. Then the teams line up and the ball is thrown in 10 yards in front of the goal without the teams changing ends. Penalty No. 2 involves a free hit from the line 30 yards in front of the goal. The defenders must stand behind the back line until the ball is hit and may not come on to the ground through the goal mouth. For penalty No. 3 a free hit is given from the line 40 yards in front of the goal, with the same restrictions on the defenders as in No. 2. Penalty No. 4 means a free hit from the line 60 yards in front of the goal. The defenders may be on the ground, but must be at least 30 yards clear of the hit. When penalty 5a is awarded a free hit is given from the place where the penalty occurred. The defenders must be 30 yards from the hit, while the attackers may be ahead of the hit. Penalty 5b is a free hit from the centre spot. The defenders must stand at least 30 yards from the hit, but the attackers may place themselves ahead of it.

Handicaps

Each player has a handicap, assessed by his national association, guided by international standards. A beginner starts his career at minus 2; the ceiling is plus 10. There are team handicaps, too, these being the aggregates of the team members' ratings. The majority of tournaments are played on a handicap basis, whereby in each match the team having the lower aggregate handicap receives a starting advantage in goals. (In studying wide divergences in scores during handicap tournaments, we are often told much about the handicapping committees' accuracy in rating individual players; or, as the case may be, about the improvement or deterioration in individuals'

4

standards of play since their handicap was last assessed.) Tournaments played without handicaps are called "open".

The term "high-goal polo" means that the aggregate handicap of a team entered for a particular tournament is, perhaps, around 19 or even higher. A 21-goal team might be composed of a Number Three with a handicap of 8, a Back with 5 and a Number One and Number Two each with 4. In Europe a high-goal team may be as low as 17, in the Argentine as high as the ultimate 40.

Beginners

Polo expertise derives far more from the combination of a natural athletic style, the unerring ability to coordinate limb and eye and a flair for ball-games in general, than it does from clever horsemanship. The successful player would invariably be good at cricket, hockey or baseball, squash, golf, *pelota* or tennis. Since polo players are obliged to wield the stick with their right hand, one who by instinct and practice holds, say, a tennis racquet or fencing weapon in his left hand, will be at a marked disadvantage as a polo player. (The author, himself thus handicapped, writes with certain feeling on the subject; it took him twice as long as most players to master the strokes and hit the ball with any convincing impact!) But if you have watched that agile performer, the American Joe Casey, a naturally left-handed man, in action, you will know how well a player thus inhibited can do.

Generally speaking it is more difficult to teach a non-ball-game player to hit a ball from horseback than it is to teach any ball-game player to ride well enough to play polo.

The beginner need not be a high-class horseman, but he must be able to concentrate on hitting without having to think about his riding, and must also be a sufficiently competent horseman to get the best out of his ponies. The same principles apply as in most other spheres of equitation. A good seat is the top requirement. This is particularly important in polo, since many shots have to be taken leaning right out of the saddle, at the gallop. The best way to achieve both firmness and balance, through strong thighs and back, is to ride regularly without stirrups, and also to do plenty of schooling exercises to keep supple at the waist and shoulder. The polo player must be capable of moving the upper and lower parts of his body more or less independently.

The polo horseman must fully understand the aids, and develop good hands as soon as possible; on the one hand he must have very good control and, on the other, generally avoid spoiling the mouth, temperament and performance of nicely-made ponies. He should be in the habit, from the beginning, of riding with his weight forward of the centre of the saddle. This is both more comfortable and less exacting for the pony and helps the player to hit correctly.

The beginner will probably learn the strokes from a dummy horse in a polo pit, a small wire-enclosed court with a sloping perimeter floor that returns the balls, and a flat centre on which is placed a wooden horse with a saddle. There are four basic polo strokes: the offside forehand, which is the equivalent of the racquets game's forehand and is the most generally used; the offside backhander, the nearside forehander and the nearside backhander. The subsidiary strokes are the forehand cut, the under-the-pony's neck shot and the backhand round-the-tail shot.

The first aim in hitting should be to develop a stylish swing, so that the stick head may properly gather momentum and the shaft guide it to the ball. The head will then expend most of its energy in driving the ball, and the remainder of it in the course of the follow-through. But the pit is inclined to give a feeling of false accomplishment, so as much practice as possible should be done from a quiet pony – as soon as possible at the canter and gallop.

Good marking implies good riding off, an art which should therefore be thoroughly practised. The ideal way to ride off an opponent is to place the knee in front of his knee, so imposing the weight of your pony a little in front of his pony and thereby steering him away from the place where the action is.

Perhaps the three priority rules for the beginner are: be a good mutual team player (don't chase the ball: man first, ball second); don't look at your pony; and don't try to hit too hard.

The beginner will, of course, take a good deal of trouble to find out precisely what equipment he needs. His helmet, his white breeches his brown boots and knee pads must all fit comfortably and (should) look smart. He will carry a whip, but spurs and a face guard are a matter of suitability.

His sticks must be very good and just the right length for him and for the pony he is riding at the time.

Tactics

The team's objective will of course be to bring the ball within striking distance of the opposition's goal-mouth. This is achieved by a combination of superior pace – fast ponies and hard galloping – sure and accurate striking, intelligent team play, alert anticipation and accurate passing.

What has been said concerning the marking of opposite numbers – the Ones versus Backs, Twos versus Threes – though a golden guideline, is not a rigid rule. The positions are essentially interchangeable. For example, if the Back is unmarked and decides he is in a favourable situation to take the ball up towards the opposition goal, the Number Three will adopt the Back's defensive role and the Number Two temporarily assume the Three's position.

While no player should have his eyes fixed anywhere but on the ball when he is going

"PLAYERS MAY IMPEDE THEIR OPPONENTS BY KNOCKING AND HOOKING THEIR STICKS." Stuart Mackenzie (8) of New Zealand, and (*right*) David Stirling (5), of Uruguay (*opposite*)

"THEY WILL ENDEAVOUR TO LEAN INTO THEM AND RIDE THEM OFF AT EVERY CONSTRUCTIVE OPPORTUNITY." Geoffrey Kent (4) of Kenya and Alex Garrahan (9) of Argentina (*right*)

for it and striking it, he must, at other times, be forever anticipating where he should next position himself; or, if in possession, judging where he can send the ball to the best advantage, endeavouring to pass it to the team-mate who has the best chance of doing something useful with it.

Although "the less shouting on the ground the better for all concerned" is an excellent principle, the following important orders are to be heard in the game: "Leave it!" "Take the man!" and "Ball!" The player who shouts "Leave it!" from behind implies that he sees a better prospect of advancing his team's interests by taking over the ball than the man in possession. Similarly "Take the man!" means "Ride off the nearest opponent, I'll take the ball". "Ball!" is translated as "You keep the ball, I'm backing you up!" These orders, which, are frequently given by the Number Three to one of his forwards, must be instantly obeyed (even although they may not always be infallibly, or judiciously, given).

The essence of good polo is "open" play (as well as clean, fair play). Open play stems from each team member adhering to his true role, marking his man, avoiding being marked, vigilantly anticipating the course of the game and developing a facility for long and accurate passes. A good team will often be seen to mount its attacks in diamond fashion by diagonal passes to the side of the ground, followed by accurate cut shots to the centre. The forwards, the Numbers One and Two will be forever contriving to place themselves in suitable positions to take up the ball, to seize the initiative for their team, and maintain it.

The four team players should, where possible, study the strengths and weaknesses of their four opponents. More important still, they should have a close mutual understanding, knowing when to interchange positions, when to cover one another and what length and accuracy of pass to expect from each team-mate. They should have plans of deployment for the hits-in and the penalty shots, whether their side is giving them or taking them. It follows from all this that they should have as much practice together as possible.

RIDING OFF IN A RACE FOR THE BALL DURING A MATCH AT CLAUDELANDS, HAMILTON, NEW ZEALAND. Jim Watson (New Zealand) in possession and (*right*) Lord Vestey (Stowell Park)

"OWING TO THE INEVITABLE HAZARDS OF THIS FAST-MOVING STICK-AND-BALL MOUNTED DUEL. . ." (*below right*)

"PENALTIES ARE AWARDED IN THE FORM OF . . . FREE HITS AT THE OFFENDER'S GOAL." Defenders anticipating a 40-yard penalty shot

"MANY SHOTS MUST BE TAKEN LEANING RIGHT OF THE SADDLE." Owen Rinehart (United States) and (*left*) Patrick Churchward (England)

Umpiring

The two umpires that every match requires wear distinctive clothing to differentiate them from the players – usually black-and-white striped shirts. There should also be a referee, who will need to have as commanding a view of the match as he can, probably in the spectator stands or perhaps the commentator's box, or, failing those, in a central position on the sideline. He will be required to arbitrate when the umpires disagree.

It goes without saying that the umpires and the referee should be intimately acquainted with the game. The first principle in umpiring is to be perpetually aware of the line of the ball and which player owns that line at every given moment of the chukka.

By the time a new player has mastered the rules and basic tactics of polo, he is ready to umpire matches fielding players of the same standard as, or of a lower standard than, himself. The tyro who gets plenty of umpiring is likely to gain a deeper understanding of the mechanics of polo than one who does not.

"THE OFFSIDE FOREHANDER, THE EQUIVALENT OF THE RACKETS GAME FOREHAND." Alfonso Pieres (9) of Argentina

THE NEARSIDE FOREHANDER. Christian La Prida (9) of Argentina

Ponies

"My old friend, Major Stanley Deed, who knew more than most people in the world about polo, especially polo ponies, was in the habit of exclaiming at short intervals during the game, 'Poor little ponies, *poor* little b——! What have they done to deserve this?'" John Board, *Polo*

"BE IN THE HABIT OF RIDING CONTINUOUSLY WITH THE WEIGHT OVER THE SADDLE." Guillermo (Memo) Gracida of Mexico, a 10-goal player

The term "polo pony" is technically a misnomer. It derives from the days before the First World War when the height limit was 14.2 hh, and before that, too, when it was under 13.3 hh. Since the most effective animal was subsequently found to stand somewhere between 15 and 16 hh, and the height limit was abolished by the Americans when Britain was at war (in 1916), the "pony" became the "horse". But "pony" is romantic to polo, traditional to the game. It is more attractive to speak of "pony power" than of "horse power", while "pony lines" is more alliterative, more redolent of polo than "horse lines". So, for the purposes of this book, "ponies" are what they are called.

Britain, with her many indigenous mountain and moorland breeds, once bred the best in the world. With the removal of the height limit and the advent on the ground of the "small horse", however, Argentina became the world's first source of good ponies, a development that coincided with the rise of that country toward international polo-playing pre-eminence. The British settlers in the Argentine, who were the pioneer players, were crossing English thoroughbreds with the most promising of their ranch mares from the end of the 19th century. Thus after the removal of the height limit,

HOWARD HIPWOOD (9) OF ENGLAND, TURNING WITH THE BALL. Hector Barrantes (Argentina), handicap 8, pulls up to avoid Hipwood's line, with Eduardo Moore, another 8-goal Argentinian, supporting behind

ATTEMPTED UNDER-THE-BODY SHOT DURING A WARWICKSHIRE CUP MATCH, CIRENCESTER, ENGLAND

increasingly good quality mares – standing some 15.2 or 15.3 hh, of the smooth, low-galloping ranch character – were produced in great numbers, by men for whom polo was, in a way, a recreational off-shoot, or spin-off from the business of ranching. I shall be saying more about all that in Chapter 4. Meanwhile, as every player is well aware, a great many equally good ponies have been bred, and continue to be bred, in the United States, the United Kingdom, New Zealand, Australia and elsewhere. There have been many ponies who were relatively poor on conformation, yet brilliant at the game. They are the exceptions that prove the rule. Good conformation – a fine natural balance, close coupling, all round "quality" – can be as important for the polo pony as it is for the competition horse or hunter. The right conformation means depth through the heart and lungs, a well rounded loin ("well ribbed up"), a straight humerus and sloping shoulder, a deep stifle, plenty of second thigh, a fairly long sloping pastern, a good length from the hip to the hock ("well let down"), strong neck and quarters, clean legs, and a round, nicely shaped foot.

Obviously, too, we are looking for animals with a kind, intelligent eye and an equable temperament to go with it – not only animals that do not "play up" during the chukka, but ponies that box and shoe and stable easily, that do not buck or kick or misbehave in the lines. All the same, it has to be admitted that some of the most useful ponies are the meanest in stable or paddock. Clearly, too, the polo pony must have a soft mouth, great courage, stamina and turn of speed.

The breeding, making and schooling of ponies is outside the scope of this book; but, to generalize, the same basic principles apply as in all other branches of "horse production''. The polo pony is long-reined, broken to the saddle and taught to go smoothly and confidently on the bit with his hocks well under him in the conventional manner. In addition he must swing very easily on those hocks, go bravely and confidently into the "ride off" and be capable of stopping dead in his tracks.

If it is a truism that sentient animals are just as prone to suffering and joy as humans are, that must be especially pertinent to such highly-bred, sensitive creatures as horses. Many polo aficionados feel a great sympathy for the ponies, seeing them clouted on the legs with mallets; quite often struck by the ball; violently jerked this way and that, with all the strain that jerking implies for the joints and tendons; and, perhaps worst of all, being frequently jabbed on the lips and bars of the mouth, particularly by bad horsemen; and all this in the throes of carrying their riders in the non-stop, high-speed marathon of a seven-and-a-half minute chukka, perhaps twice in the afternoon.

It is not good enough to say, with a shrug, that the rest of those polo ponies' lives consist of luxury stables, gentle exercise and the best fodder that money can buy. Pain and discomfort are unpleasant and the more they can be avoided the better. For this reason ponies are never played without boots or bandages, even at stick-and-ball, and their saddles and bridles should be carefully checked for comfort before fitting. The good player always inspects his ponies for injuries after a game. If a pony is going badly the last thing the owner/rider should do is to condemn it as "idle" or "bloody-minded". Sensing that it is suffering in some way or other he will check its teeth and legs and the fitting of its tack. (Is the tree of the saddle in good shape? Was the curb chain fitted correctly? Is the girth chafing? etc.) If necessary he will call in a vet without delay.

OWEN RINEHART (9) OF THE UNITED STATES, TAKES THE BALL UNDER HIS PONY'S TAIL. He is followed by Lionel Macaire (France) and (*right*) Alan Kent (England)

The player

Here, reprinted from the 1984 Palm Beach and Country Club programme, is an essay by the world's senior performer, Juan Carlos Harriott:

"The tradition of the polo player as a truly international sportsman has been building up over the past century as polo spread around the world. Especially during the past 50 years, as modern transportation and communications brought us closer together, this tradition has gained strength. Polo players are able to travel with their own teams to compete in other countries, or as individuals to join the teams of other countries for a season. Even the player who never leaves home may have friends from almost every corner of the world where polo is played. Whether he has a handicap of 10 goals or one, the player shares in this tradition, in the international friendships, in the high standard of sportsmanship which for me is what makes this game great. Every generation has the responsibility to preserve this tradition.

"Polo is not a gentle game. There is risk and danger involved. Perhaps it is this which binds us together most strongly, which has created such a high standard of comradeship and sportsmanship. We know that if each of us was not a gentleman out on the field, we would injure one another.

MARTIN BROWN (ENGLAND): NEARSIDE UNDER-THE-NECK

14

ALFONSO PIERES (ARGENTINA): OFFSIDE UNDER-THE-NECK DURING THE 1985 WORLD CUP. He is challenged by Ben Taub (United States), of the Boehm team

"IMPOSE THE WEIGHT OF YOUR PONY A LITTLE IN FRONT OF HIS PONY." Alfonso Pieres in possession again with Christian La Prida, a fellow Argentine 9-goaler

15

"INTELLIGENT TEAM PLAY, ALERT ANTICIPATION. . . ." Stefan Macaire (France), third from the right, in possession of the ball for Los Locos in their 1985 Warwickshire Cup final

"To preserve our tradition requires from every player a sense of dedication to the game. I am not saying that the average player has to devote as much time and effort to polo as the high-goal player or that to enjoy the game he must always strive for perfection. The broad base of world polo is made up of many thousands of low-goal players from many countries (and even those who hold no rating or who do not have the advantage of being registered with a national association). These players are as important to polo as those with higher handicaps who are able to compete in the major tournaments. We must not forget that the high-goal players of tomorrow will come from among the thousands of low-goal players today, and even those players who may never get the chance to increase their handicaps still make an essential contribution to polo through their enthusiastic support of the game. They are in every sense important members of our international polo community.

"The basic spiritual approach of every player, however, whatever his handicap, must include that strong sense of dedication of which I speak if he is to be considered a good player within his capabilities.

"Polo is a sport which should be played with hot blood and a cool head. When you go out on the field to start the first chukka, you must be prepared to fight straight through to the last bell and whistle. This means you must be prepared both physically and mentally to uphold your quarter of the game, always remembering that you are only one of four men in your team and that you are not playing for yourself, but for your team. If you are lucky enough to have *presencia*, a presence which inspires confidence, as well as a good team spirit, then you can be an even greater advantage to your team.

"A polo player must have character, not so much physical courage – although this is obviously not a game for the timid – but the heart to fight back when you are down. In Argentina we call this *garra*. Even a top player has his bad days, when he seems unable to hit the ball or to be in the right place at the right time or

16

THE PRINCE OF WALES FOLLOWS THROUGH WITH AN OFFSIDE BACKHANDER

"SENTIENT ANIMALS CAN BE JUST AS PRONE TO SUFFERING, AS WELL AS JOY, AS HUMANS ARE"

to do anything right. On such a day, a player has to have the *garra* to keep on fighting. It is this courage which can bring victory to a team even though they have been outplayed by their opponents.

"I must stress again the need for sportsmanship in a polo player. A man who is a bit of a prima donna and plays for himself rather than for his team cannot be a good player. A player who rides onto the field ill-prepared for the class of polo he is playing or who lacks the proper concern for the safety of his team-mates and opponents, or a player who deliberately commits a foul to gain an advantage, is dangerous. He can cause accidents which can be crippling or even fatal to both men and horses. He should not be allowed on the field. Fortunately for polo such players are very rare indeed.

"If a player has the right character for polo, as I have discussed above, then there are certain things he can do to improve his game, to increase his handicap and to get greater enjoyment from the sport.

"A good polo player must be in good physical condition. For many of us in Argentina, this presents no great problem because we work on ranches and play polo 10 months a year, not always big competitions, of course, but mostly "country polo" at small clubs. Even when there are no games, we usually work on horseback, and can take an hour or so off to stick-and-ball on the *estancia*.

"For others who do not live so much with horses it is necessary to find a complementary sport to keep in good shape outside the polo season. For example, when I am not able to work out with the ponies, I play squash to keep my eye and speed and wind up to the mark.

"You must be a good rider in order to cover the field, to be where you should be to hit the ball or to take out your man, and to conserve your horse during the

18

MEMO GRACIDA TAPPING THE BALL FORWARD WHILE RONALD FERGUSON (*left*) ATTEMPTS TO INTERCEPT

game. Style and horsemanship are important too, and add to the beauty of the game, but most important is to be a good natural rider.

"You must have the right attitude toward your pony, I think it is difficult for a man who does not love his horse to be a really good player. The ideal, of course, is to be able to breed and make your own ponies, but whether you have this added pleasure or must buy your ponies, you must treat them with respect and love. The pony will respond to such treatment and will help you to play better polo. When you are on the field there is not time to think consciously about your pony. You must concentrate on the game. This means that you and the pony should be as one.

"You must have speed, of course with the help of a good pony, and you must be able to hit well. Always remember that a well hit ball travels faster than any pony, so try to hit hard and true if not to the goal then to a team-mate who is in a better position than you.

19

"Anticipation is essential for a good polo player, anticipation of your team-mate's moves as well as those of your opponents. Good anticipation can often make up to some degree for a lack of speed. Sometimes a man with a slower pony can reach the ball more quickly than an opponent who is better mounted, by anticipating the action.

"Finally, one of the greatest advantages to a high-goal player anywhere in the world is to feel the stimulation of major competition. Whether he is able to play polo 10 months a year or only during a short season, he needs to feel the excitement of important competition to realize his full potential. A good enthusiastic crowd of supporters can help to create this atmosphere, but in the end whether you are playing before a crowd of 3,000 or 30,000, it is the cup that you and your team are fighting for. The bigger the cup, the stiffer the competition, the better the player you become."

That, briefly, is what polo is about – and what it means to take up the game. Now we shall turn back through the pages of history to see where and how it all began, how "modern polo" developed and the place it assumes in the world today.

"GOOD CONFORMATION CAN BE AS IMPORTANT FOR THE POLO PONY AS IT IS FOR THE COMPETITION HORSE OR HUNTER." Spice, the property of Galen Weston (Canada), to whom Her Majesty the Queen handed The World of Sport Trophy after Julian Hipwood had ridden the pony in the 1985 match for England's International Coronation Cup

20

PERSIANS AT PLAY

G. D. ARMOUR'S IMPRESSION OF PERSIANS AT PLAY

THE GREAT JOHN WATSON

WOMEN AT PLAY IN ANCIENT CHINA

Chapter 2

FROM EAST TO WEST

Man is a Ball tossed into the Field of Existence, driven hither and thither by the Chaugán-Stick of Destiny, wielded by the hand of Providence.

Metaphor of ancient Persia

Pageantry and an aura of elegance surround the most important polo matches of today. Heralded by military bands, trumpeters and equestrian displays, they take place amid the dazzle and glitter of bunting and flags. The smart turn-out of the players and their ponies and the sartorial efforts of the spectators are echoes of the game as it was played in the ancient East.

Over 2000 years ago in ancient Persia in the lands that bestrode the valleys of the Tigris and Euphrates polo was known as *chaugán*, a "mallet". It was the sport of aristocrats and cavalry officers just as it was when it developed in England towards the end of the 19th century. The artists of old Persia, the cradle of polo, loved to depict the game as an equestrian ballet performed before the king attended by an orchestra of pipes and drums, a ballet in which brightly uniformed attendants hold spare sticks for the equally dapper players. The poet Firdusi described the opening of a game in *Sháh-nama*, *Book of Kings*, which has been referred to as the *Iliad* of Persia and was dedicated to the Sultan Mahmud of Ghazna in 1010 A.D.

> "Then the band began to play and the air was filled with dust. You would have thought there was an earthquake so great was the noise of trumpets and cymbals. Then the king started the game by throwing in the ball in the correct manner."

If the historian Tabári is to be believed polo was already an old tradition by the time of Alexander the Great. Tabári records how the Persian King Darius Codomannus (*c.* 370–330 B.C.) refused to pay his customary tribute to Alexander, and how, when the young Macedonian threatened invasion, Darius sent him a chaugán stick and ball suggesting that playthings were more suited to Alexander's immaturity and inexperience than the weapons of war. Alexander replied with characteristic sharpness: "The ball is the earth and I am the stick". He went on to defeat Darius at the battle of Gangamela in 331 B.C., and Darius was put to death a year later.

21

POLO, OR *CHAUGÁN*, PLAYED BEFORE THE SULTAN MAHMUD
OF GHAZNA, IN THE PERSIA OF THE EARLY 11TH CENTURY. The
picture is taken from Firdusi's *Sháh-nama* (Book of Kings)

Moving on a thousand years to recount the life of the Caliph of Baghdad, Haroun
al-Raschid (763–809 A.D.), Tabári remarks that at one important point in the ruler's
youth he was "still so small that, when on horseback he could not reach to strike the ball
with his chaugán". Firdusi took much poetic licence in his writings on polo. Describing
a match between seven Persians and seven Turks, he states that the Persian Siáwasch, a
"10-goaler" of his day, strikes the ball so hard that "it almost reaches the moon", while
another star player, Gushtasp, wields his chaugán with such effect that "the ball could
no longer be seen by any person on the *maidán* (plain) as his blow had caused it to
vanish amongst the clouds." Another Persian poet, Nizami of Ganja (1140–1202)
recounts how the lovely Shírin, wife of Khusran Parviz the Victorious, played chaugán
with her ladies-in-waiting against the king and his courtiers:

> *On one side was the Moon and her Stars*
> *On the other the Shah and his Firman-Bearers.*

The historian Cinnanus shows Comnenus (Alexius I, the Byzantine Emperor, 1048–
1118) enjoying chaugán with his princes and nobles, their ball being "of stuffed leather,
the size of an apple . . ."

"This is the game, then, [Cinnanus continues] a very doubtful and dangerous
one as he who would play it must be constantly lying flat on his horse, and
bending himself on either side of his horse, and be turning his horse very
sharply, and he must manage to ride so as to be skilled in moving his body and
his horse in as many different ways as the ball is driven."

22

◁ From East to West ▷

Jámi, in his narrative poem *Salámán and Absal*, which was written in about 1414, conjures a picture of the youthful Salámán at polo:

> *All young in years and courage, bat in hand,*
> *Galloped afield, tossed down the golden ball,*
> *And chased so many crescent moons a-full,*
> *And all alike intent upon the game.*
> *Salámán still would carry from them all*
> *The prize, and shouting 'Hál!' drive home the ball.*

A century or two later we find the greatest of the Mogul emperors, Akbar (1542–1602), a devotee of the game. His chief minister, Abul Fazil, wrote in his exhaustive work, *Akbar Nameh*: "His Majesty, who is an excellent judge of mankind, uses these sports as a latent means of discovering their merits." The three English Sherley brothers, visiting Akbar's court, were straightaway impressed with the performances they saw played on well-kept and carefully levelled grounds, but conducted in a very rough-and-tumble manner. "There were twelve horsemen in all with the King," wrote the brothers' secretary, George Manwaring,

> "so they divided themselves six on one side, six on the other, having in their hands long rods of wood about the bigness of a man's finger, and at one end of the rods a piece of wood nailed on like a hammer. After they were divided, and turned face to face, there came one in the middle, and threw a ball between the companies, and, having goals made at either end of the plain, they began their sport, striking the ball with their rods from one to the other, in the fashion of our football here in England . . ."

A later Englishman to witness the game, Sir William Ouseley, mentions it in his *Travels in the East* (1810):

> "It was universally practised throughout Persia, and was a favourite recreation of kings and chiefs, and originally, I believe, considered as almost peculiar to illustrious personages. The object of those who played was to drive through the goal with sticks having semicircular or straight transverse heads a ball made of light wood, which the contending parties – governed by certain prescribed laws, and striking only when at full gallop – endeavoured to bear off one from the other. Of this game there were several kinds, and I perceive in the pictures of manuscripts executed two and four hundred years ago that the *chaugáns*, or sticks, are represented with heads of three slightly different shapes."

From Persia and other parts of the Near East the game spread to China, and, in the 6th century, from China to Japan, where it was known as *diaku*, meaning "strike the ball". An 8th century reference to the game which occurs in Basil Hall Chamberlain's *Classical Poetry of the Japanese*, runs as follows:

> "In the first moon of the fourth year of the period Zhiúki (727 A.D.) the nobles and courtiers had assembled in the fields of Kasuga, and were diverting themselves with a game of polo, when the sky was suddenly overcast and the rain poured down amid thunder and lightning."

Polo almost died out in Japan in the 19th century during the rebellion that ended the feudal system, but by the 1880s it had been revived. An eye-witness account of the game in a *Times* report of 1889 included the following description:

"The arena is a flat grassed rectangle, 216 ft long and 60 ft wide . . . All the balls are made of paper with a cover of very small pebbles and bamboo fibre. Their diameter is 1.7 inch, and they weigh very nearly 1¼ oz. Each rider carries a light wand, called *kiu-tsui*, of tapering bamboo, only about ½ inch in diameter at the thick end and 3 ft 8 in long. To its extremity is bound a flat, narrow strip of bamboo, bent over so as to form a semicircle of 1.5 inch radius, the outer end of which is held in position by a silken stay passing obliquely down to the bamboo shaft, 2 inches from its head . . . On each side, red and white, there are an equal number of players – usually from six to eight – distinguished by the colour of their headdress, and the object of each side is to get a certain number of balls into the net at the goal . . . The signal for the game is given by the umpire and echoed by a brisk peal from the gong and drum. The riders, previously drawn up at the starting-point, now press forward with the balls as thrown in to them by the attendant behind the rails. Carrying, passing, casting – any means providing that the *kiu-tsui*, or stick, only is used – are allowed for getting the balls forward, until they are finally pitched into the net from the hither side of the goal railing."

15TH-CENTURY CHINESE PAINTING ON SILK OF MONGOLS AT PLAY. The composition is thought to be based on an original of the Yuan dynasty (1280–1368) when China was under Mongol rule

Although the game was popular among the Mogul emperors of Hindustan up to the 16th century, there are no known references to polo in the Indian sub-continent during the 17th and 18th centuries. Be that as it may, it was picked up from the Chinese by the Tibetans, who named it *pulu*, their word for a ball; and it was most likely from Tibet that the people of Manipur – that mountainous state sandwiched between Assam and

A MANIPURI TEAM AS THEY WOULD HAVE LOOKED WHEN THE EUROPEAN TEA-PLANTERS LEARNED THEIR GAME IN THE 1850s

Burma – adopted the game. The Manipuris called it *kán-jāi-bazèè*, but they knew it, too, as *pulu*, the word that so comfortably adapted to make our title for the game.

Each group of Manipuri villages had its simple polo game and club. In 1854 tea planting was started by Europeans in the Manipuri valley of Cachar and some of the planters soon joined in the sport. A subaltern in the Bengal Army, Lieutenant Joseph Sherer, also played his first game of *pulu* with the Manipuris in 1854. After the Mutiny he and Captain Robert Stewart, Superintendent of Cachar, founded the first European polo club there in 1859. Joe Sherer was to become known as the Father of Western Polo. Here he is as Major-General Sherer recalling his memories of Manipuri polo when the game had taken root in many other parts of India:

> "To see *kán-jāi-bazèè* played in its greatest perfection one should go to the fountain-head of the game, at the Munnipore capital itself. I took my team up there in 1865, and the Maharajah got up several matches for me. I and my band who had been so proud of our victories in Calcutta, were simply *nowhere* in Munnipore. We never won a single game. The game was fast and furious. The Maharajah's men were his picked team, the best players in the State – clean, clever, and scientific in their strokes and sharp as needles. The Munnipooris, again, were no respecters of persons. It was quite permissible, and recognized as lawful, to ride *at* and *through* anything or anybody that came between the player and the spot where the ball lay. I was once caught in this position and dilemma, and was simply sent spinning, pony and all, and got considerably shaken and bruised."

25

In 1861 Stewart's brother, Captain G. Stewart of the Guides Cavalry, having accumulated a number of sticks and balls, formed clubs at Barrackpore and Cawnpore. In 1863 the game reached Tonghoo in Burma. In 1864 Captain Kinloch of the Rifle Brigade, one of India's better-known big-game hunters, having seen and played polo at S'rinagar, the capital of Kashmir, brought it down to Meerut, north-east of Delhi, where his regiment and the 19th Hussars took it up. By 1865 the game was firmly established in Bengal, by 1867 in Madras and by 1870 throughout British India.

Polo continued to be played as it was played in old Manipur in many remote corners of India at least until the Second World War. Here is an account by Charles Chenevix Trench, a former Indian cavalryman, in his book *The Frontier Scouts*.

"The game to which all the tribesmen, including of course the Scouts, were passionately addicted was polo. Not the polo of Delhi, Smith's Lawn or Cowdray, but the game which was played in Central Asia for many hundreds of years. In the 1940s a spate washed away a gravel bank in the Kuh-Ghizr river to reveal a Dedication Plaque announcing that the King had opened a polo ground, with all the proper rites, nearly two thousand years ago.

"It was played in every village, and every town; the ground was long and narrow, perhaps two hundred yards by fifty, but in villages it might be the village street. Every man between fifteen and fifty who owned or could borrow a pony played. It is not everywhere that polo is seen as a social leveller; but in Kuh-Ghizr or Ishkoman there might be seen Rajah, shepherd, British officer, Scouts sepoy, and all the ragtail and bobtail of the valley playing together in perfect good fellowship and indifference to person, galloping about in a cloud of dust and enjoying themselves enormously. The best ponies, of about fourteen hands, were imported from Badakshan or the Russian Pamirs and in the 1930s cost about 200 rupees. All were stallions, which added a new dimension to the game. To keep them sound, they were 'yorrocked' before and after a match. This consisted of taking a horse for a short exercise canter, and then standing him in a water-channel, saddle on, girth loosened, head exaggeratedly over-bent, until he had staled twice. It was very effective – and needed to be, for in the traditional village polo a chukka continued until nine goals had been scored, though in Gilgit where alien influence had crept in, chukkas were limited to half an hour. In village games there was no limit to the number of players, but in more formal matches they were restricted to six a side.

"There were no rules against crossing or foul-hooking. After a goal had been scored, the scorer enjoyed a free hit, known as a 'tambuk'. Galloping down to the half-way line, he leant forward holding the ball beside the horse's right ear and then, with a terrific underhand sweep, hit it towards the enemy goal. It was not unusual for an expert to hit three goals in successive tambuks. Another very skilful ploy was to hit the ball against the stone wall which bordered the ground, catch it as it bounced back and gallop with it through the goal while the opposition did all it could to get the ball off the striker or the striker off his horse. The famous frontier doctor, Lloyd Ledger, performed the now legendary feat of vaulting on to the ball-carrier's horse at full gallop and, riding pillion behind him, steering the horse willy-nilly through his own goal.

"The game was seen at its best at the annual *jhalsa* in Gilgit when the Mirs and Rajahs assembled for homage to the King Emperor (and, perfunctorily, to the Maharajah of Kashmir), to pay a small tribute in gold-dust washed from local rivers, and to receive gifts such as a sporting rifle or a telescope, with Scouts Guard of Honour and all the populace looking on. Polo matches between kingdoms – Hunza *v*. Nagar, Punial *v*. Yasin were the great features of the occasion. In the morning the Scouts' drums and pipes would play in the 'Commanding Sahib's' garden announcing to the world that there would be polo that afternoon. By half-past two all the Mirs and Rajahs, if not actually playing, would be seated in a shamiana on the west wall of the ground. Opposite them were positioned the bands of the respective teams. (Some ponies were such sticklers for custom that they would not perform without music.) The Political Agent opened the game by throwing in the ball, and then it started, fast and very furious, all the best players competing fiercely for the honour of their states while the bands played louder and louder, rising to crescendo as a goal was scored or saved. Feelings ran high, and on more than one occasion the Political Agent had to stop a match lest blood be shed and a blood-feud result. When a match was over, the losers had to dance before the winners, a ceremony which was tactfully omitted when British officers were in the vanquished team."

It has been stated and repeated more than once that the game reached England through the introduction of a regiment, or regiments, lately stationed in India. Considering the germ of polo entered the British *Raj* in 1854 and spread rapidly through the Army of India during the 1860s, it is somewhat surprising that those assertions are erroneous. It is a well documented fact that the origin of the game in Europe can be traced to a cavalry mess at Aldershot in 1869. T. A. St Quintin, a witness to the event, remembers the day in his *Chances of Sports of Sorts*:

"It is ancient history now that one day in 1869, when the 10th Hussars were under canvas at Aldershot for the summer drills, 'Chicken' Hartopp, lying back

CHANGING PONIES DURING A MATCH BETWEEN THE ROYAL HORSE GUARDS AND THE 17TH LANCERS

THE OLD PAVILION AT RANELAGH

was appreciably faster. As Miller remarked: "Although our English ponies have more speed than the Indian ones, the ball travels faster and easier in India, and players are continually trying to overtake the ball at full pace there, instead of steadying for it as in England."

Many of the Indian rulers became great enthusiasts from the start, notably the Maharajahs of Cooch Behar, Mysore and Jodhpur. The Nizam and nobles of Hyderabad maintained professional teams, but Moray Brown was sceptical about their

POLO PONIES. H. Lucas-Lucas

RAWALPINDI, 1881: AN INTER-REGIMENTAL. R. E. Galindo

MEETING THE BALL. Isidore Bonheur

WHAT AN ARTIST AT THE TURN OF THE CENTURY
THOUGHT ABOUT THE PROSPECT OF WOMEN
PLAYERS: *POLO BEWITCHED,* by Cuthbert Bradley

THE OLD PAVILION AT PHOENIX PARK, DUBLIN, BUILT WHEN THE GROUND WAS LAID DOWN IN THE 1870s.
Posed in front are the Co. Sligo team who won the County Cup on six occasions around the turn of
the century. (*Left to right*) H. L'Estrange, P. Connolly, Major C. K. O'Hara and J. Fitzgerald

members: "They lack combination, however, and each man plays too much for himself.
It is a pity that one of these teams does not visit Hurlingham and see if it could hold its
own against such players as the Messrs Peat, John Watson, etc." But very soon Indian
players came on the scene who were every bit as good as the top English performers.
The best in the 1890s were Sir Rajinder Singh Mahinde and H.H. the Bahader of Patiala,
and their laurels were inherited by Moti Lall of Alwar and Dhokal Singh of Jodhpur.

Perhaps the greatest name to come out of Anglo-Indian polo was that of General Sir
Beauvoir de Lisle, who captained the seemingly invincible Durham Light Infantry team
in India during the 1890s. "Mr de Lisle is a most enthusiastic player," Moray Brown
said of him as a subaltern; "indeed report affirms that when not actually playing polo
on a live animal, he sits on a wooden horse for hours, hitting balls as they are thrown at
him and practising every sort of stroke." Paying tribute to him when he was Colonel de
Lisle, Miller wrote: "Indian polo players owe him a debt of gratitude for having proved
to them the possibility of playing on first-class ponies in first-class company for almost
nothing. He has shown them that a team of novices can by practice, care, keenness and
discipline, be brought into the very front rank." Winston Churchill who played with
the 4th Hussars, gave a very good idea, in *My Early Life* of how much of the life of a
cavalry officer serving in India was taken up with the game:

"We three, Reginald Barnes, Hugo Baring and I, pooling all our resources, took a
palatial bungalow, all pink and white with heavy tiled roof and deep verandahs
sustained by white plaster columns, wreathed in purple bougainvillaea. It stood

37

THE SELF-CHUKKER.

Mr. Churchill has retired from the Business
Committee of the Conservative Party.

(Rare piece of the Mogul School; Eighteenth Century).

in a compound of grounds of perhaps two acres. We took over from the late occupant about a hundred and fifty splendid standard roses: Maréchal Niel, La France, Gloire de Dijon, etc. We built a large tiled barn with mud walls, containing stabling for thirty horses and ponies. Our three butlers formed a triumvirate in which no internal dissensions ever appeared. We paid an equal contribution into the pot; and, thus freed from mundane cares, devoted ourselves to the serious purpose of life.

This was expressed in one word – Polo. It was upon this, apart from duty, that all our interest was concentrated. But before you could play polo, you must have ponies. We had formed on the voyage a regimental polo club, which in return for

HURLINGHAM CLUB HOUSE

THE MAN WHO TOOK POLO FROM ENGLAND TO AMERICA: JAMES GORDON BENNETT

moderate but regular subscriptions from all the officers (polo-players and non-polo-players alike) offered substantial credit facilities for the procuring of these indispensable allies. A regiment coming from home was never expected to count in the Indian polo world for a couple of years. It took that time to get a proper stud of ponies together. However, the president of our polo club and the senior officers, after prolonged and anxious discussions, determined upon a bold and novel stroke. The Bycullah stables at Bombay form the main emporium through which Arab horses and ponies are imported to India. The Poona Light Horse, a native regiment strongly officered by British, had in virtue of its permanent station an obvious advantage in the purchase of Arabian ponies. On our way through Poona we had tried their ponies, and had entered into deeply important negotiations with them. Finally it was decided that the regimental polo club should purchase the entire polo stud of twenty-five ponies possessed by the Poona Light Horse; so that these ponies should form the nucleus around which we could gather the means of future victory in the Inter-Regimental Tournament. I can hardly describe the sustained intensity of purpose with which we threw ourselves into this audacious and colossal undertaking. Never in the history of Indian polo had a cavalry regiment from Southern India won the Inter-Regimental cup. We knew it would take two or three years of sacrifice, contrivance and effort. But if all other diversions were put aside, we did not believe that success was beyond our compass. To this task then we then settled down with complete absorption.''

Going back to the year 1876, when Churchill was a lad of five and polo in England was only seven years old, an American newspaper tycoon paid a significant visit to England. 1876 was the last year of tenure of General Ulysses S. Grant, Union hero of the Civil War, in the White House; it was the year in which General Custer made his mortal stand against the Sioux Indians at Little Big Horn River, Montana; it was, too, the year in which James Gordon Bennett saw polo played at Hurlingham and took it home to the United States.

39

Chapter 3

AMERICA AND THE WESTCHESTER

The Winning Goal

What though 'twas luck as much as skill that gathered up the pass,
Before us lies an open goal and eighty yards of grass.
Now all ye gods of Hurlingham, come hearken to my call,
Give pace unto the twinkling feet that fly before them all.

Their back is thwarted on the turn; their three's out-thrown and wide;
Their one and two can scarce get through, however hard they ride;
So stretch your neck, my swift Babette, and lay you down at speed,
There's not a flier on the field can rob you of the lead!

The dancing ball runs straight and true, the ground is fast as fire;
To us remains the single stroke to crown our heart's desire.
With purple on their ponies' flanks they close on either side,
But you will keep in front, Babette, whose only spur is pride.

One drive to make the trophy ours! One glorious goal to get!
The slow ball hangs and curves away. Swing in! Swing in, Babette!
Now! How the tingle of the stroke through arm and shoulder spins!
A hefty hit . . . a deadly line . . . a goal! the goal that wins!

Will H. Ogilvie

James Gordon Bennett Jr, son of the founder of the *New York Herald* and himself proprietor of that newspaper, has been described as "a tyrant", whose employees "were terrified of him". But he was an entrepreneurial journalist of considerable imagination. Bennett was the Editor-in-Chief, who, in his long and sensational career sent H. M. Stanley, in 1871, to find Dr Livingstone; in 1874, bore half the cost of Stanley's Congo expedition; in 1879, arranged the U.S. Navy's Arctic expedition in *Jeannette*; and, in 1873, promoted the Commercial Cable Company – all magnificent grist to the *New York Herald* mill. He was also, in the opinion of the American polo historian, Newell Bent, "one of the best and most liberal patrons of sport our country has ever known." In regard to his visit to Hurlingham in 1876, the plutocratic, patrician, physically fit image of the young officers appears to have delighted him as much as their new "Hockey on Horseback" itself:

> "The men who played the game impressed this American tycoon immensely. They were the cream of the British army: bronzed centaurs, hardened from years in the saddle, racing, foxhunting and troop duty. They were wealthy (no one in the British cavalry would ever try to live on his salary, which was impossible, anyway) and sports-minded, but full of the hearty good fellowship of athletes."

Returning to the United States with a plentiful supply of sticks and balls Bennett immediately dispatched New York's leading riding master, Harry Blasson, to Texas to purchase suitable ponies. Before 1876 was out he had staged his initial demonstration game – in "old Dickel's" indoor riding academy on the corner of 5th Avenue and 39th Street. The precursors of American polo, having spent much of the winter of 1876–7 trying out ponies and practising their shots, proceeded, in the following spring, to Jerome Park racetrack, Westchester county, where they held their first series of outdoor games, with Bennett and the American-domiciled Lord Mandeville as captains of the two sides.

1886: THE FIRST WINNERS OF THE WESTCHESTER CUP. (*Left to right*) Capt. John Watson, Capt. Thomas Hone, Capt. Malcolm Little and Capt. the Hon. Richard Lawley. Their umpire, Capt. the Hon. Charles Lambton, stands behind

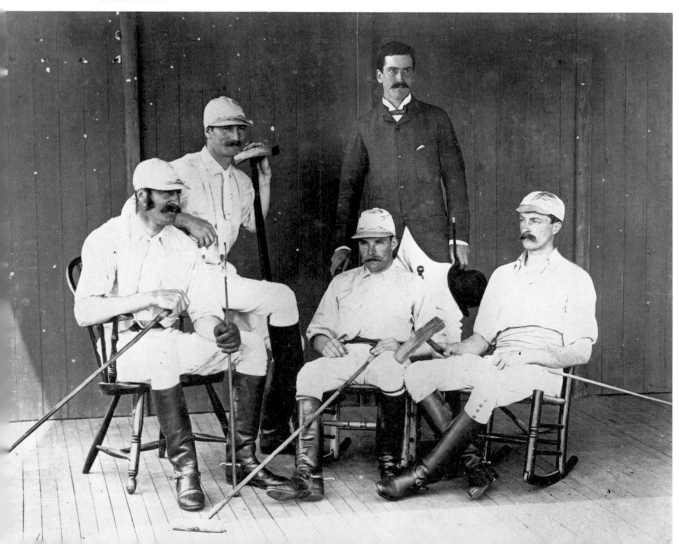

H. L. HERBERT, CHAIRMAN OF THE U.S. POLO ASSOCIATION (1890–1921). Sitting on the fence: Mrs A. Belmont Purdey

Bennett, who had given the game to his country, complete with the Hurlingham rules, sold his ponies and withdrew from the scene to his numerous other interests in 1878, but the flame which he brought spread with a steady glow. 1879, which saw the sprouting of a crop of new clubs, was a vintage year for American polo. A group of players based on the Mineola fair ground on Long Island, formed what later gave rise to the legendary Meadow Brook Club. Inaugurated in 1881, it grew to be America's Hurlingham. Then August Belmont established the Queen's County Club, and H. L. Herbert, who would be the first chairman of the U.S. Polo Association in 1890 and the Grand Old Man of the game, formed the Brighton Club, his first club sticks being "croquet mallets, lengthened with hayrake handles." Another prominent name in American polo is that of W. A. Hazard, who was the Association's first Honorary Secretary and Treasurer.

In 1878 a pitch was marked out on the Military Parade Ground at Prospect Park, Brooklyn, and on June 21, 1879, America's first public match – a five-a-side affair lasting 80 minutes with the umpires on foot – was played there, with 10,000 spectators flocking to see "the new English game". This was between Westchester and Queen's County. Belmont and Herbert played for Westchester, while in the Queen's County team appeared a name that was to resound in sporting America, Tommy Hitchcock. This was, of course, Thomas Hitchcock, Sr, who had learned the game as an Oxford undergraduate. Herbert recalled the contest: "Team play was then unknown and the

42

hero of the day was the individual who could score the greatest number of goals, regardless of the others on the side. The play consisted mostly of a huddling, pushing, shouting mass, and few had the skill to race away with the ball.''

It was the British challenge that was to weld the American team, ''the Big Four'', that would, a quarter of a century hence, be the best in the world. Griswold Lorillard, of the Westchester, dining at the Hurlingham Club one evening in the spring of 1886, remarked casually to his hosts that polo was played in the United States. ''The statement was met with surprise'', said Lorillard's club secretary, F. Gray Griswold, ''and the suggestion was made that if the matter of expense could be shared, a team from the Hurlingham Club could perhaps go across and play a series of matches with the Westchester Club.'' Lorillard cabled Griswold, who replied that ''all expenses of a team and its ponies will be met and the Westchester Polo Club will offer and have made a cup, to be emblematic of a polo championship of the two countries.''

1886

The Hurlingham team, under the captaincy of John Watson, was completed by Captains the Hon. Richard Lawley and Thomas Hone, 7th Hussars, and Malcolm Little, 9th Lancers. These four, with their umpire Captain the Hon. Charles Lambton, duly sailed for New York on the Cunard liner *Servia* on August 7, their ponies having embarked earlier in the *Erin* (and enjoyed a much calmer passage). The Englishmen travelled on to Newport, Rhode Island, the Westchester's summer resort, where they were warmly welcomed by their opponents, Thomas Hitchcock, Raymond Belmont, Foxhall P. Keene and W. K. Thorn. In a series of matches, composed of three chukkas

AN AMERICAN TEAM OF THE 1880s: THE ROCKAWAY HUNTING CLUB. (*Left to right*) J. D. Cheever, H. L. Herbert, W. Rutherford, Foxhall D. Keene and John Cowdin

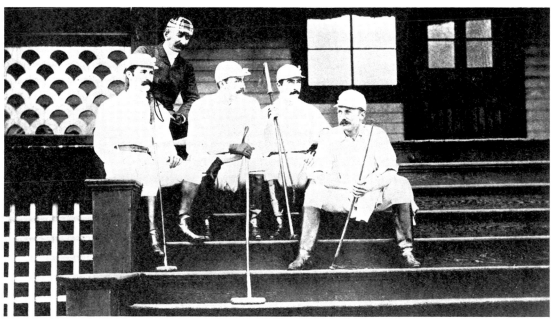

SPECTATORS AT HURLINGHAM AT THE TURN OF THE CENTURY

most complete knowledge of the game of polo." The spare man was Louis Stoddard, another distinguished poloist in the making.

Whitney borrowed the best available ponies, 28 in all and saw to it that they were brought to the peak of condition and maintained in that condition. Larry Fitzpatrick held the important post of "Master of the horse". Cottontail, Cinders, Mallard, Flora, Cinderella, Grayling, Cobnut, Summer Lightning and Kitty were some of the names – many of them well-known English ponies – that shone in the American string.

Himself a brilliant Number Three, Whitney trained his selected squad according to their positions on the ground; he taught them, too, the effective flexibility of interchanging those positions and of the essential practice of long passing, well co-ordinated attack and accurate goal shooting. He developed polo into as fast a game as had ever been seen. Nor, when his men reached England and began their practice games, did he let up for a moment. "He had a stentorian voice," said Foxhall Keene, his predecessor in the American captaincy,

> ". . . and not only the players but everyone for miles around knew just what he thought at all times. He was in command always, never stopped talking during the game and played the team as though it was a unit obedient to his brain. . . . When he captained a team he worked at it. He kept strict tabs on his players to make sure they kept training rules, chasing the Waterburys and Milburn around London like a headmaster after schoolboys and making sure they got in at a reasonable hour each evening."

England fielded Captain Herbert Wilson, Frederick Freake, P. W. Nickalls, Lord Wodehouse, Harry Rich and Captain J. Hardress Lloyd (Wilson – and Wodehouse who was called upon at the last minute in place of C. D. Miller – only taking part in the first match and Rich and Hardress Lloyd only in the second). In the traditional Westchester "best of three" matches, consisting of six periods of ten minutes each, played on the

50

ENGLAND VERSUS IRELAND, HURLINGHAM 1910

23rd of June and the 5th of July, the Americans won outright, 9–5 and 8–2. "Mr Whitney had brought with him a team which showed for the first time the possibilities of combination and discipline in a free galloping game," wrote T. F. Dale in *Polo at Home and Abroad*. "The first thing that struck English polo players was the wide intervals between the American players, and their long passes. . . ." So Whitney's strategy paid off *par excellence* and amid great rejoicing, the Westchester was taken home for the first time. *The Times* correspondent reported:

"It may be said at once that the better team has won. British ponies were outplayed and our team didn't play together. Their hitting was a treat to behold and the faster they galloped, the more certain were their shots. Their instinct of the exact position of the goal when driving their ponies at top speed was never at fault, and they made a wonderful percentage of goals in proportion to their openings. Time and again when the English team had worked the ball down to the American back line, Mr L. Waterbury or his brother would obtain possession of the ball and take it the whole length of the ground, driving it in front of them with a certainty and accuracy which were beyond praise.

"The hope that it would be missed at the second or third shot always proved delusive and Mr L. Waterbury's run in the fifth chukka of the first game when he took the ball the whole length of the ground and wound up with a brilliant goal was a marvellous piece of play.

"Mr Milburn's backhanders were a source of infinite strength to his side, and the way he drove them on both sides of his pony right through the game up to his forwards had much to do with the success of his side.

"The Englishmen were outponied and had had no practice together. The Americans owe success entirely to the brilliance of their attack, which, thanks to their splendid ponies and wonderful quick and strong hitting, they developed to perfection."

51

ENGLAND'S CHAMPION PRIVATE TEAM OF 1910: THE OLD CANTABS. (*Left to right*) Frederick Freake, Lord Wodehouse, Capt. G. Belville and Walter Buckmaster. (Freake, Buckmaster and Wodehouse all achieved 10 handicaps.)

1911

England, knowing that the next battle for the Westchester must be on American soil, and therefore to be played under American conditions, now suspended the offside rule, all their practice from then on being without that inhibition. With a determination born of national pride, in the spring of 1911 Captain Hardress Lloyd and his three teammates arrived in the United States to bid for the cup which John Watson's team had first captured exactly a quarter of a century before. They proceeded first to Georgian Court, Lakewood, for their practice games, then, in June, to the Rockaway Club at Cedarhurst for the Tournament. Hardress Lloyd, positioned at Three, was supported at One by Captain Leslie Cheape (soon to be hailed as "England's greatest player") at Two by Captain Noel Edwards and at Back by Captain Herbert Wilson. The reserve was Captain "Rattle" Barrett. The team took with them 35 ponies, 14 of those being bought by the American Cup Recovery Fund Committee and the remainder loaned by Lord Ashby St Legers, Lord Dalmeny, the Duke of Westminster and other British players. But many of the ponies were too young and green, and says Bent, "proved something of a failure, so much so that Captain Lloyd had great difficulty in mounting his men properly when the matches were finally played in June."

Not so the Americans who collected together a substantial number of well-tried mounts, "Offers coming from all over the country," Bent tells us, "placing at Mr Whitney's disposal, ponies, sometimes whole stables of ponies, to be used for any purpose he deemed advisable. Mr Walter Dupee, of California, for instance, sent eight of his best ponies three thousand miles to Lakewood, feeling himself amply rewarded when Alverne and Berta, both Californian-bred were played by Mr L. Waterbury. Once again the American mounts were all under the watchful eye of Larry Fitzpatrick, who gave them their final schoolings before the matches."

The Americans kept their 1909 line-up – Whitney, Milburn and the two forward-playing Waterburys – now known as the "Big Four". Their spare men were Foxhall Keene, Louis Stoddard and Malcolm Stevenson. Even so the Americans, the holders of the Westchester, were hard put to keep ahead, and, in two straight matches – each of eight chukkas of 7½ minutes – were only victorious by the narrow margin of 4½–3 and 4½–3½.

THE "BIG FOUR" – THE AMERICAN WESTCHESTER SQUAD OF 1911: (*Left to right*) Devereux Milburn, Harry Payne Whitney, Monty Waterbury Jr and Larry Waterbury

1913

Undaunted, a Hurlingham team returned for a new Westchester series in 1913, this time mounted by the Duke of Westminster, "who left nothing undone to get together forty-two of the finest ponies procurable". Walter Buckmaster, who should have been the English captain, was put out of action from a bad fall in the spring. So Captain R. G. Ritson led the 1913 British invasion, with Captains A. N. Edwards, Vivian Lockett and Leslie Cheape filling the other positions, and Frederick Freake in reserve. Lockett, of the 17th/21st Lancers, was a prominent cricketer as well as a fine polo player. Moreover, he enjoyed a reputation in Leicestershire as "an exceptionally good man to hounds".

The organization of the United States quartet that year was fraught with drama. First Monty Waterbury broke his finger and was replaced by Louis Stoddard. Then, as the "Big Four" had been playing badly in the 1912 season, Harry Payne Whitney resigned the captaincy in favour of the veteran Foxhall Keene. Deprived of Whitney's leadership Larry Waterbury decided to pull out. So the line up was to have been Stoddard, Milburn, Keene and Stevenson. Subsequently Freake fell and broke his collar-bone in a practice match, Monty Waterbury's thumb mended and the team that showed up was the "Big Four"! – except that Louis Stoddard (who proved a great discovery as a Number One) substituted for Monty Waterbury in the second match. A neck-and-neck struggle – the closest Westchester tournament ever played – ensued. The Americans employed the rushing attacks they had displayed in 1911 and snatched a lead they never relinquished. In the second match each side made five goals, while each was penalized half a goal for crossing. The final result hinged on ¼ of a goal penalty for a "safety" which Ritson was obliged to make to prevent a goal against his team, the score being 5¾–5½ to the U.S.A. Dev Milburn was the man of the tournament. He played three of his best chukkas off the back of the celebrated brown English gelding, Tenby. G. D. Armour, himself a poloist, who was covering the 1913 matches for *Country Life* in his capacity as an artist, had some interesting things to say in his autobiography, *Bridle and Brush*:

"Milburn's play was always a joy to watch, and some of his defending shots marvellous. He could loft the ball over everyone's head half-way up the ground, either forward or backward, as I don't think I have ever seen done by anyone else. Both the Waterburys were strong, good hitters, and very certain at all angles before goal, and I think Whitney, the captain, was also exceedingly capable in that respect.

"In connection with the first match, I was particularly struck with this – certainly surmise also – that in practice games the American captain had probably noticed that our men were rather given to starting slow – that is, of course, comparatively speaking – and warming up in pace as things developed, and had given instructions to his men to go all out from the throw-in. Be this as it may, they put on two goals within two or three minutes of the start, and it appeared to me, kept the ball out of the middle line of the ground and play as far as possible afterwards.

"It struck me that the big four were not pretty horsemen, not, at least, so good to look at as our own. But even this they seemed to turn to good account, their forward seat enabling them, sometimes, to hit some most difficult shots round the fore-end of their ponies. L. Waterbury hit one of their goals in this way, when appearing almost to sit on his pony's neck. I think, also, they were rather given to taking chances.

HARRY PAYNE WHITNEY LEADING THE VICTORIOUS "BIG FOUR", IN BRONZE, BY HERBERT HASELTINE

CAPT. NOEL EDWARDS, ENGLAND'S NUMBER TWO, TAKES A BACKHANDER DURING THE 1911 WESTCHESTER CUP. (*Left to right*) Larry Waterbury, Edwards, Monty Waterbury, Devereux Milburn and Capt. Hardress Lloyd

"All round, I think they were better mounted than our men, had faster ponies, and, of course, had then, as now we also have, no size limit. The matches were played in tremendous heat, beneath a literally brazen sky, which was very trying for all concerned. Those in authority allowed me to see the games from the boards, or anywhere I wished, not perhaps the best view to have of the whole points of the game but offering me a chance to see details of it more useful from a pictorial point of view, and without obstruction from such things – if I may say so – as the expansive hats which ladies then used to wear.

"I think the American influence speeded up polo as it did racing, and I am sure that the pace at which these international games go necessitates those taking part being in the youthful prime of life and absolutely fit to stand the strain entailed, to say nothing of the ponies."

Between 1891 and 1914 the following were awarded 10-goal handicaps. From the USA: Foxhall Keene, Rodolphe Agassiz, Thomas Hitchcock Sr and Larry and Monty Waterbury. From England: "Rattle" Barrett, Leslie Cheape, E. W. E. Palmes, R. G. Ritson, Walter Buckmaster, J. Hardress Lloyd, Vivian Lockett and Lord Wodehouse.

FREDERICK FREAKE, ENGLISH WESTCHESTER TEAM MEMBER 1902 AND 1909

CAPT. LESLIE ST C. CHEAPE, ENGLISH WESTCHESTER TEAM
MEMBER, 1913 AND 1914. He was killed on the Turkish front
in the Great War

WALTER BUCKMASTER, CAPTAIN OF THE OLD CANTABS, AND
THOUGHT BY MANY TO BE THE FINEST ENGLISH PLAYER IN THE
YEARS BEFORE THE GREAT WAR. He would have captained his
country's Westchester team in 1913, but for injury

CAPT. R. G. RITSON IN POSSESSION OF THE BALL DURING THE 1913 WESTCHESTER. (*Left to right*) Cheape,
Whitney, Ritson and Milburn

1914

Hurlingham was prompt to challenge again. The English 1914 squad was comprised of Cheape, Lockett, Barrett and a new name, Captain H. A. Tomkinson. Johnny Traill, from the Argentine, should have been included, but at the last was unable to be present. Cheape's sister having just died he postponed his crossing until one trial match before the opening of the series. Then, just as he began playing, he received a flying ball smack in the face, and suffered a broken nose. The Americans generously agreed to a four-day postponement, after which delay Cheape gallantly reappeared. Lord Wimborne turned up trumps by producing a splendid lot of ponies and English hearts soared higher on hearing the news that Whitney – the man they regarded as "the most level-headed poloist we've ever played against" and "the quickest polo thinker" – had retired from tournament polo. In the event the American line-up was René La Montagne (Back), Monty Waterbury (Three), Devereux Milburn (Two) and Larry Waterbury (One). Moving Milburn up to Two was patently a mistake, and England proved it by winning the first match 8½–3. For the second Milburn changed positions, and, at one point, America was in the lead. But the British team of 1914 was distinctly superior; in particular Tomkinson made a dashing goal-scoring debut as their Number One, and they triumphed again, 4–2¾.

And so the people who were the founders of modern polo, represented by the strongest foursome they had ever produced, carried home the Westchester Cup. Then they went to war, and – with anything in mind but a fresh international polo challenge – for the next four years they fought the Germans. Cheape, commanding a squadron of the Worcestershire Yeomanry, was killed in a battle with the Turks on Easter Sunday, 1916. And at least one rising star from the United States failed to come out of the conflict unscathed. That was Thomas Hitchcock Jr who began playing polo at the age of 6 and who was to take the centre of the stage in the polo world of the post-war years. Turned

MEADOW BROOK, 1914. Parade of ponies in front of the west stand prior to a Westchester match

down for the American Air Force on account of his youth, he joined the French Lafayette Escadrille, quickly qualified as a pilot, got shot down over the German lines, spent four months in hospitals and prison camps, jumped from a prisoners' train near Ulm and foot-slogged it by night compass to Switzerland and safety. By 1921 he was representing his country in the next return Westchester.

Five years earlier the Americans, by shelving the 14.2 hand height rule, had changed the complexion of the game somewhat and British poloists returning from the trenches were faced with a *fait accompli*. But that belongs to another chapter. Meanwhile polo had long been blossoming in other lands. It is time to turn back to the 1870s and see how all that came about.

WESTCHESTER SPECTATORS, 1914. Mrs F. W. ("Rattle") Barrett, John Traill (the Anglo-Argentine player), Lord and Lady Wimborne and Mrs Traill. Lord Wimborne provided most of the English team's ponies (*top left*)

THE WESTCHESTER CUP (*top right*)

WINNERS OF THE INDIAN POLO ASSOCIATION CHALLENGE CUP, 1907: THE RAJPUTANA PILGRIMS: (*standing*) Their Highnesses Sewai Maharajah Jey Singh of Alwar and (*right*) Kanwar Moti Lal of Alwar; (*sitting*) His Highness Maharajah Madan Singh of Kishangarh and an unidentified player

THE DUKE OF WESTMINSTER'S TEAM. (*Left to right*) Capt. the Earl of Rocksavage, Capt. Riversdale Grenfell, the Duke of Westminster and Capt. Francis Grenfell. The Grenfell twins, who were also in the 9th Lancers team with Lord Rocksavage, were both killed in the Great War, Francis Grenfell winning the V.C.

Chapter 4

HOW THE TORCH WAS CARRIED AFAR

Beneath the rainbow silks they sail
Like birds that wheel and cross;
Then, all their speed of no avail,
Come round to bit and martingale
With heads that reach and toss.

The ceaseless stick beside them swings,
The torn turf marks their track,
To heaving flanks the dark sweat clings
And from their fretted bridle rings
The foam comes feathering back.

But well they know there is no game
That men their masters play
Can fan like this their hearts to flame
And make them one with every aim
That fills the crowded day.

Will. H. Ogilvie

Argentina

Englishmen were the initiators and pioneers of modern polo; English sportsmen, more than any other people, were the harbingers of the game through the western world; and Englishmen first played it in the country which has been, since the 1930s, by general acclaim, the world's leading polo nation – Argentina.

From 1877, the year in which Mr Shennan began playing with his friends on his *estancia* at El Negrete, the other great cattle ranchers eagerly took up the game. In 1883 the Flores Club was founded on the outskirts of Buenos Aires; in 1880 came the Lomas Club, and, in 1889, the Hurlingham Club, with two very important names among its members, Frank Balfour and Hugh Scott-Robson. In 1892 (by which time there were more clubs in the country than there were in Britain) the various committees formed the

THE SHOT FROM THE GREY PONY. From the painting by Gilbert Holiday. Note the left-handed player on the right of the picture

Polo Association of the River Plate which remained Argentina's governing body until 1923.

The leading Argentine polo family of the early days was that of Traill. The North Santa Fé team was composed for a time entirely of Traills, the most famous of whom

61

New Zealand

Witchery

Rich bay with a star on the face
And white on the off hind-foot
With a beautiful temper and plenty of pace
And keen as a hawk to boot.
With a shoulder as clean as a stag's
And loins that would carry a ton,
There's nothing so kindly goes down to the flags
As Witchery – fourteen-one.

She's a wonder at getting away,
And give her a length on the grass,
They can bid a good-day to the swift little bay,
For there's nothing can catch her or pass;
She fights for her head to the ball,
For the ponies are fond of the fun,
And oh! but she loves to be leading them all,
Does Witchery – fourteen-one.

Girth up, and ride out to the fray!
For our foemen in crimson and white,
They are demons to play and they mean it today:
We shall have to hit hard and sit tight.
And we've got to take risks of our own
When the coin has been spoken and spun,
And the hard knocks, remember, are not all alone
For Witchery – fourteen-one.

Anon. New Zealand

In February, 1888, *HMSs Opal, Swingle, Nelson, Diamond* and *Calliope* put into Auckland, in New Zealand's North Island for the opening of the Calliope Dock. Several of the officers who had learnt polo in Malta, took sticks and balls ashore and showed the residents how the game was played. Teddy O'Rorke, son of Sir Maurice, Speaker in the House of Representatives, suggested to the keen local equestrian fraternity that "we ought to have a go at this sport!" Several of his friends found suitable ponies and picked up the rudiments of it from the sailors. Thus, that summer, the Auckland Polo Club was formed.

O'Rorke, bursting with enthusiasm, travelled to South Island where he soon got his Christchurch friends interested. A British Army officer, Lieutenant R. S. Savile, ADC to the New Zealand Governor, the Earl of Onslow, suggested an inter-club national trophy and promptly presented one, the Savile Cup. This was first played for between the Auckland and Christchurch clubs at Auckland in 1890, the umpires being

THE FIRST NEW ZEALAND TEAM TO TAKE ON AUSTRALIA: (*Standing*) A. Strang, S. Williamson, W. Strang. (*Sitting*) J. Strang, A. Baker, O. Robinson

Lieutenant Savile and *HMS Opal*'s Lieutenant the Hon. H. Tyrwhitt. The New Zealand Polo Association was formed in 1898.

Following the recession of polo in New Zealand during the First World War the tournament for the Savile Cup was revived in 1920, the most important link between pre-war and post-war being in the person of Robert L. Levin. It was Levin who organized the country's first national ground – on the oval of the Fielding racecourse. Starting as a playing member of the Wellington Club he became secretary in 1904 and was elected onto the committee of management four years later. He was vice-president of the Association in 1925, President in 1926 and Patron in 1947. Before the First World War there were nine active clubs in New Zealand; by 1929, greatly owing to his enthusiasm, another seven had been added.

Australia

The game has an even older tradition in Australia. According to Moray Brown, Captain St Quintin, 10th Hussars and his brother introduced polo to the Antipodes in 1876. A few years later, on the invitation of the Governor, Sir Hercules Robinson, the first ground was laid out at Sydney, whose equestrian citizens then formed a very active club. By the early 1890s the game was popular as far afield as the island of Tasmania, as the equestrian poet, A. B. ("Banjo") Paterson tells us in his verses "The Geebung Polo Club":

It was somewhere up in the country, in a land of rock and scrub
That they formed an institution called the Geebung Polo Club.
They were long and wiry natives from the rugged mountain side,
And the horse was never saddled that the Geebungs couldn't ride;
But their style of playing was irregular and rash —
They had mighty little science, but a mighty lot of dash:
And they played on mountain ponies that were muscular and strong,
Though their coats were quite unpolished, and their manes and tails were long.
And they used to train those ponies wheeling cattle in the scrub;
They were demons were the members of the Geebung Polo Club.

It was somewhere down the country, in a city's smoke and steam,
That a polo club existed, called "The Cuff and Collar Team".
As a social institution 'twas a marvellous success,
For the members were distinguished by exclusiveness and dress.
They had natty little ponies that were nice, and smooth and sleek,
For their cultivated owners only rode them once a week.
So they started up the country in pursuit of sport and fame,
For they meant to show the Geebungs how they ought to play the game;
And they took their valets with them — just to give their boots a rub
Ere they started operations on the Geebung Polo Club.

Now my readers can imagine how the contest ebbed and flowed,
When the Geebung boys got going it was time to clear the road;
And the game was so terrific that ere half the time was gone
A spectator's leg was broken — just from merely looking on.
For they waddied one another till the plain was strewn with dead,
While the score was kept so even that they neither got ahead.
And the Cuff and Collar Captain, when he tumbled off to die
Was the last surviving player — so the game was called a tie.

Then the Captain of the Geebungs raised him slowly from the ground,
Though his wounds were mostly mortal, yet he fiercely gazed around;
There was no one to oppose him — all the rest were in a trance,
So he scrambled on his pony for his last expiring chance,
For he meant to make an effort to get victory to his side;
So he struck at goal — and missed it — then he tumbled off and died.

By the Old Campaspe River, where the breezes shake the grass,
There's a row of little gravestones that the stockmen never pass,
For they bear a rude inscription saying, 'Stranger, drop a tear
For the Cuff and Collar players and the Geebung boys lie here.'
And on misty moonlit evenings, while the dingoes howl around,
You can see their shadows flitting down that phantom polo ground;

◁ *How The Torch Was Carried Afar* ▷

You can hear the loud collisions as the flying players meet,
And the rattle of the mallets, and the rush of ponies' feet,
Till the terrified spectator rides like blazes to the pub –
He's been haunted by the spectres of the Geebung Polo Club.

CHRISTCHURCH, THE FIRST WINNERS OF NEW ZEALAND'S SAVILE CUP. (*Left to right*) A. W. Bennetts, G. J. F. Palmer, A. E. G. Rhodes and R. H. Rhodes

Paterson witnessed the game as a guest of the Royal Navy in 1892. The Earl of Glasgow, whose father was Governor of New Zealand and who was then serving as Midshipman the Viscount Kelburn, on *HMS Curacao*, remembered the occasion for posterity in the 1950s:

> "With regard to the poem 'The Geebung Polo Club', A. B. Paterson was our guest on *HMS Curacao* and came with us from Sydney to Hobart. The game was played up country (not at Hobart) against some very tough Tasmanian farmers. With eyes like hawks they seldom missed the ball but their knowledge of the rules was rudimentary! Wherever the ball went they made for it and crosses were frequent. I don't want to exaggerate but certainly one arm was broken as the result of a collision between ponies. I remember seeing, as the result of

71

TWO FAMOUS AUSTRALIAN TEAMS OF THE EARLY 1900s. (*Standing, left to right between the umpires*), Sydney: Colin Stephens, Jack Garvan, Tom Watson and Jock Morton. (*Sitting*) The Manifold Brothers of Victoria

another collision, the pony of Lieutenant Vivian de Crespigny going in circles with de Crespigny dismounted being dragged over the ground holding on to the bridle. It was the roughest game I have ever seen and Banjo was there and witnessed it."

Breeders in New South Wales were supplying horses to the mounted elements of the Indian army since well before the end of the 19th century. Known as "Walers" this hardy and handy breed made useful polo ponies, too. Regarding the usefulness of Australasian stock in general, E. D. Miller wrote:

"In Australia, New Zealand and Tasmania there are a large number of well-bred galloping ponies, which are essentially of English blood, and which differ but little from the home product. They are generally well up to weight, and are coming into fashion enormously in India, where they have quite superseded Arabs as first-class tournament ponies.

"Colonel de Lisle, a great Indian polo player, and Captain of the Durham Light Infantry Polo Team, is a warm admirer of Australasian ponies, and prefers them to all others for polo in the East. He owned a pair of beauties and tells me

"It was in 1922 during a visit to India by the Prince of Wales, himse
polo player. He offered a cup for a tournament held in his honour. The
between my team, Jodhpur, and a team we had never beaten, the grea
which had won everything up until the First World War and was still
after the war.

"Imagine the scene in Delhi: a crowd of 150,000 people around the p
among them the future King of England, the Viceroy, some 50 mahara
princes, dozens of generals and high government officials and all t
dressed as if they were to be received at Court. Such an atmosphere
added to our determination to win. My father had set his heart on this
we had a string of 150 ponies from which to choose. Patiala had eve
resources, including a style of polo that I can only describe as a ches
wonderful control of the ball from all corners of the field. We knew the
to beat them was with a game of speed, always playing the ball to an i
line straight down the centre of the field from one goal to another. T
way we played, but Patiala was still leading 4–0 in the third chukka
scored just before the interval, and after the interval we caught fire
even with Patiala and, in the final minute of the match, passing them.
from the crowd were so deafening that none of us heard the final bug
knew the game was over only when thousands of spectators began pou
the field. As my No 1, Prithi Singh, rode past the V.I.P. pavilion, he
stick round and round his head and threw it high into the air. Dignit

RAO RAJAH HANUT SINGH

that they were quicker starters, and faster, than Arabs. These Australasian
ponies, with all the good points of English ponies, have legs and feet able to
stand galloping on hard ground. As a rule, Australasian ponies have less bone
than English ponies; but they can carry weight."

The early Australian players were well mounted and also well instructed by their
English mentors, starting with the St Quintin brothers. The young cavalry officer
serving in India during the 1880s who drew up the "polo code and hints for players" for
New South Wales was Captain Douglas Haig, one day to be famous as Field-Marshal
Earl Haig, commander of the British Army on the Western Front. By the mid-1920s
there were 25 clubs affiliated to the Polo Association of Australia and the game was
played all the year round at Sydney. In the two post-war seasons New South Wales's
Goulburn team, composed of the four Ashton brothers, went with their New Zealand
ponies and "Walers", first to England and then on to the United States, putting up a
very creditable performance in both countries.

Europe and Africa

Meanwhile polo had long been established in most parts of the European continent,
particularly in France, Germany, Italy, Spain, Hungary, Poland, Russia and Austria. In
nearly every sphere in which the white man settled in Africa clubs were formed, and
already it was a national sport in Kenya, the Rhodesias, Nigeria and the Gold Coast.

The game was first played in South Africa at King Williamstown in 1875, the teams
being drawn from the Gordon Highlanders, the Duke of Cornwall's Light Infantry and
the Cape Mounted Rifles. Polo began in 1903 in Kenya, where the first ground was laid
out on Naiborbi Hill opposite the old King's African Rifles barracks. Ghana's Accra Polo
Club was founded in 1902. Its birthplace in Nigeria, in 1904, was Lagos and, in 1914,
Kaiser Wilhelm II presented a cup for a championship between Nigeria and the German
Cameroons. Polo started even earlier in Rhodesia, where it was launched at a meeting
of the Salisbury Sports Club in December 1896.

The Singapore Club must be the oldest surviving foundation. Established in 1866, on
the initiative of officers of the Buffs, polo was first played there on a ground 300 yards
long by 80 yards wide opposite Raffles Hotel.

Chapter 5

THE GOLDEN YI

Rao Rajah Hanut Singh

We are now launched into the 1920s and '30s, years in w
glamorous or more skilfully or dashingly played. They we
taxation and widespread support for the game. No polo
unselfish sportsmanship or the high standard of polo that w
than Rao Rajah Hanut Singh. Born in 1900 and strictly l
father, Sir Pertarb Singh, Hanut's polo education commenc
less an instructor than Dhokal Singh who was probably Ir
time. In 1914 Sir Pertarb mobilized his State cavalry and
France. Hanut became the youngest officer the Jodhpur L

Emerging from the grime and horror of the Western Fr
1918 to play in the next Delhi tournament off a handicap
raised to 8, and, in 1919, to 9, the rating which he kep
thought he should have represented Britain against the I
Westchester series in 1921, 1924, 1927 and 1930; but the Hu
he was too small and light and would be too easily bumpe
Americans. Hanut did not agree. ''My ponies were so f
slipped them every time,'' he said with his smiling shrug,
'bumping' air!'' He was eventually invited to play for th
but injury prevented him from taking part.

Let us return with him, however, to 1922 and see hov
greatest match I ever played in''. His team – Jodhpur – ca
six teams, to meet Patiala, a 36-goal squad in the final of
Prince of Wales, then touring India, presented a cup:

> ''Players often ask me what I consider the greatest m
> during more than half a century of polo. Before my
> played around the world from Calcutta to Deauv
> Meadow Brook. I have played with or against all th
> rank as the truly great players. Even after all t
> international polo, I would still choose as my greatest
> place almost 50 years ago in India.

74

the pavilion rushed out onto the field to capture the stick as a souvenir. It was a
scene I will never forget, but what I remember most was the reaction of my
father, who died later that year. I think Sir H. Perry-Robinson, writing in *The
Times* of London, described the end of the game better than I can: 'Halfway
through the chukka Jodhpur scored and drew even at five-all. Three more
minutes to go, and through those minutes men, important major-generals and
personages in high political office, stood up in the grandstand waving their hats
and shouting themselves hoarse, and women screamed. Only one figure it
seems sat motionless. In front of the stands sat Sir Pertarb Singh, Regent of
Jodhpur and grand old polo player. He is I believe 78 years old now and sits on
his horse still beautifully. And all India knows that the Jodhpur team is the very
apple of his eye, his darling and his pride, and he had coaxed and nursed it for
this fight. Through all this game he sat immovable, not a muscle not an eyelid or
a finger moving. Not even in that last demoniac minute when Jodhpur scored its
sixth goal and won. He was a figure carved out of wood. Then as the horn
sounded people from all sides broke, cheering and tumultuous, to congratulate
him, the Prince among the first. And as the old man stood up, tears poured
down his cheeks.'''

''*Now* I can die happy!'' Those were the ecstatic words of Hanut's father when at last he
spoke. And his son went from strength to strength. From 1931 to 1939 he captained the
Jaipur team, which was beaten only once in the Indian Championship in all those years,
and which won the Hurlingham Championship Cup in 1933. As C. P. J. B. observed in
Polo Monthly:

> ''A fair, if inadequate, description of the 1938–39 season in India could be written
> in five letters: H-A-N-U-T. The player whose name these letters denote has been
> famous throughout the polo world for the last 18 years. . . . It has been a good
> season. That it should have been dominated by Rao Rajah Hanut Singh merely
> shows its good taste. Hanut has won all the prizes the Eastern hemisphere has to
> offer. . . .''

Although Hanut's post-war career rightly belongs to the next chapter, it would be
fitting, in this cameo, to print a tribute to him that was paid towards the end of his polo
career. Here is Sir Andrew Horsbrugh-Porter, the former international player who was
polo correspondent to *The Times* in the 1960s and '70s:

> ''It was always from Number Three that Hanut organized his teams, seldom
> hitting goals himself, but, with that unforgettable cut-out shot from the
> sidelines, placing the ball twenty yards in front of the goal for his Number One to
> tap through. . . . Hanut thinks deeply about all aspects of polo and no one
> knows more about how to school and produce ponies and players. I think his
> finest achievement in later life was to win the Cowdray Park Gold Cup for Eric
> Moller's Jersey Lilies in 1964 and 1965. Hanut selected three unknown young
> players and collected and supervised the ponies. He was himself then rated at 4
> goals, but his brain-power was still equal to his old 9-goal handicap, and his
> meticulous management of the ponies was based on many years of experience.
> For he was quite the best judge of potential polo ponies of his generation. . . .
> You never saw Hanut having to put pressure on the reins – a delicate touch and
> the pony responded. Likewise he could suit ponies to players. . . .

76

REDS VERSUS WHITES. G. D. Rowlandson

LIGHT BLUE VERSUS DARK BLUE. G. D. Rowlandson

HURLINGHAM PAVILION.
H. Jamyn Brooks 1890

KEY

1 J. E. Peat, Esq.
2 T. S. Kennedy, Esq.
3 F. B. Mildmay, Esq., M.P.
4 Alfred Peat, Esq.
5 Earl of Harrington
6 Captain Julian Spicer, Royal Horse Guards
7 W. A. Elin, Esq.
8 Captain Smithson, 13th Hussars
9 Captain R. Chaloner, 3rd Hussars
10 A. E. Batchelor, Esq.
11 W. H. Walker, Esq.
12 Percy J. Browne, Esq., Royal Dragoons
13 J. M. Walker, Esq.
14 Unidentified
15 Arthur B. Hesham, Esq., Royal Dragoons
16 Captain C. R. Burn, Royal Dragoons
17 F. Y. MacMahon, Esq., Royal Dragoons
18 E. W. Baird, Esq., 10th Hussars
19 Captain J. Barry
20 Hon. W. F. North
21 Captain L. W. Jones
22 Captain C. Williams, 13th Hussars
23 John Watson Esq.
24 Captain Thomas Hone
25 W. H. Peat, Esq.
26 Captain W. Smythe
27 Ross
28 Captain F. Colvin, 9th Lancers
29 Captain J. H. Lamont, 9th Lancers
30 Codrington F. Crawshay, Esq.
31 J. R. Walker, Esq.
32 Gerald H. Hardy, Esq.
33 Peter Walker, Esq.
34 J. Howard Cartland, Esq.
35 Seymour Vandeleur, Esq., Scots Guards
36 Major Peters, 4th Hussars
37 George A. Lockett, Esq.
38 Captain Jenner, 9th Lancers
39 Sir Humphrey F. de Trafford, Bart.
40 Cecil Grenfell, Esq.
41 F. L. Vaughan, Esq.
42 Captain J. A. Orr-Ewing, 16th Lancers
43 H. C. Bentley, Esq.
44 F. C. Meyrick, Esq., 11th Hussars
45 Henry Dundas, Esq., 15th Hussars
46 E. Kenyon Stowe, Esq.
47 Arthur Peat, Esq.
48 A. Suart, Esq.
49 Captain Little, 9th Lancers
50 H. P. Bird, Esq.
51 E. A. Bird, Esq.
52 J. Moray Brown, Esq.

A MATCH IN FRANCE.

DEVEREUX MILBURN. Sir Alfred Munnings

"Once when he was playing holiday polo at a French resort behind a Number One who needed a bit of Dutch courage, Hanut dosed him with brandy and they won the match. Afterwards the Number One said: 'I saw two polo sticks, two polo balls, four ears on my pony and two Hanuts!' At which Rao Rajah drew himself to his full height and replied: 'There is only *one* Hanut!'

"He represents all that is best in the old Rajput aristocracy, which taught the British the way to play polo."

Hanut was still playing off a handicap of 3 when he retired to his home at Ratanada at the age of 72.

Demise of the Westchester

Whether or not the inclusion of Hanut in the English Westchester teams would have made an appreciable difference to that country's fortunes between the wars, the British poloists never really recovered from the setback of the Great War, and they never won the Westchester again. There was more to it than the single cause of having put the game behind them for four years. For one thing they were short of top-notch performers. Among the British players who had taken part in international matches and who died in the conflict, besides Leslie Cheape, were the Grenfell twins, Rivy and Francis, Captain H. Wilson and Captain Noel Edwards. Dozens more young poloists who had been coming on strongly, in 1914, also gave their lives.

English polo faced new financial difficulties, too. As the Americans grew richer, so the British became poorer. While British polo had contracted since its Edwardian heyday American polo grew fast in the 1920s. To name but two spheres of expansion, Carl G. Fisher made Florida a popular winter resort for polo players, and many Texas ranchers took up the game, emulating their counterparts in the Argentine. The Americans, while finding more and more good young players to draw upon, were able to pay huge prices for the best Argentine ponies, prices often prohibitive to the war-impoverished British. Nonetheless, both sides were anxious to see the revival of the Westchester.

1921

These verses by Will H. Ogilvie were printed on the menu card of the dinner given in London by *The Field* before the 1921 series:

Our Guests

We welcome you,
Our guests from o'er the sea!
Together flew
Our flags till the world was free;
And now they shall fly for us while we ride
In our rival friendship side by side.

◁ *The World of Polo* ▷

With you we share
The love of the Greatest Game
Played clean and fair
With no reward, but fame –
Fame and the Anglo-Saxon pride
In a goal to get and a horse to ride.

Win we or lose
Clinch firm our vantage or fail,
Your galloping shoes
Our hearts are glad to hail;
And here's a health to the Big Twin Lands –
Speed to our ponies! Skill to our hands!''

SPECTATORS IN 1921. The Earl of Rocksavage (afterwards 5th Marquess of Cholmondeley) with (*right*) the 10-goal Westchester Cup player, Capt. R. G. Ritson. The caption to this photograph, in Lord Rocksavage's album, reads: "Self, broke collar-bone, knocked over by Milburn, stopped chance playing for England"

For this first post-war international England's foursome comprised the three survivors from their 1914 squad, Lockett, Tomkinson and Barrett – and Lord Wodehouse (who succeeded as 3rd Earl of Kimberley in 1932), now a 10-goaler. They were mainly mounted, as England's 1914 squad had been, by Lord Wimborne.

The United States fielded Devereux Milburn (hailed as "the greatest Back there's ever been"); J. Watson Webb, a left-handed player (who, among other talents enjoyed a considerable reputation as an amateur huntsman and breeder of hounds); Louis Stoddard (so often described as "that great personality"); and, of course, Tommy Hitchcock Jr. A war veteran of the Escadrille Lafayette when he was still only 20 years old, Tommy Hitchcock Jr was the son of a Westchester father and of a mother who captained her own team (Old Aiken) and introduced many boy players to the game. Hitchcock Jr, the American "golden boy", was to be the lynchpin of American polo and of whom many pundits later opined: "His handicap should be 12, not 10!" With what has been described as his "great charm and dynamic presence", Hitchcock, who was to hold a 10 handicap for 18 years, became the *beau ideal* of a generation of young Americans entering the game.

The great convention at that time was that play should take place on the holders' grounds, so the Americans sailed to England. Determined to retrieve the cup they wintered their ponies there and took endless pains to perfect their team tactics. In two straight duels they won 11–4, 10–6.

> "Nobody had expected such a crushing defeat for the home team," [wrote an observer of the first match]. "The winners gave a brilliant all-round display, Mr Milburn doing wonderful things, considering that, having sprained himself in the practice games, he was playing under difficulty. Mr Watson Webb surpassed himself, the youthful Mr Hitchcock was also a great success, while Mr Louis Stoddard was seen to much advantage on Belle of All and his other exceedingly fast ponies. . . . Up to the end of the fifth period of the second match, it was either side's game. While America led at that moment by 8 goals to 6 they had not had any the better of the general run of the game. . . . Chance after chance of scoring was thrown away by the home side. . . ."

1924, 1927 *and* 1930

In 1924, at Meadow Brook, the Americans were easily victorious, the scores being 16–5, 14–5, and the teams drawn from the following:

USA – J. Watson Webb, Thomas Hitchcock Jr, Malcolm Stevenson, Devereux Milburn, R. E. Strawbridge Jr; England – Major T. W. Kirkwood, Major F. B. Hurndall, Major E. G. Atkinson, Luis Lacey, Lt-Col T. P. Melvill, Major G. H. Phipps Hornby.

In 1927, polo in the British Raj having reached new heights, the Hurlingham committee more or less delegated selection to the Army in India Association, who came forward with the following names: Major E. G. Atkinson, Captains J. P. Dening, R. George, C. E. Pert, C. T. I. Roark and Major A. H. Williams. (Of these, Captain John Pitt Dening, 11th PAVO Cavalry, was one of polo's more colourful characters. Widely known as "Dening Sahib", he was the pivot of his regimental team, which won the Indian championship in 1928. He suffered from malaria and also headaches from three bad polo falls, after one of which he was unconscious for a week. Whilst on leave in

TOMMY HITCHCOCK JR AND HIS FATHER, THE 1880s WESTCHESTER PLAYER, IN THE 1920s

April 1929 he shot himself in a London hotel on account of "a desperate love affair".) The ponies, a high quality collection of English, Argentines and Indians, many of which were lent by the Maharajahs of Jodhpur and Ratlam and Captain the Hon. F. E. Guest, were placed in the care and management of Lieutenant-Colonel George de la Poer Beresford. The Maharajah of Ratlam accompanied the team as adviser, going with them for their preliminary practice to the Westchester-Biltmore Club at Rye, New York. Pert, Williams, Roark and Atkinson played in the first match, George and Dening replacing Pert and Williams in the second. The Americans put on the same team for both matches: Milburn, Stevenson, Hitchcock and Webb. They won 13–3 on September 10th and 8–5 on September 14th. Newell Bent records:

"No team that has ever visited our shores has ever shown more pluck, courage and determination than did this British side in this second game for it was as good a team as any that has ever crossed the water. . . . In the second game, there occurred one of those fine acts of sportsmanship that so frequently stand out in these matches between England and America. With several periods to play and the game anybody's, Mr Stevenson was hurt by a flying ball, which caught him squarely on the kneecap, paralysing temporarily his whole left leg. Painfully hurt he came back into the game at the end of some 10 or 15 minutes and was met by Captain George with an enquiry as to which leg was the injured one. On being told, the English player pulled around and throughout the desperately played remainder of the game, in spite of the important advantage that was his, never once bumped or rode Stevenson off on his near side. . . . Looking back on our long years of international polo, the 1927 American line-up, with its smooth team play and tremendous power, must go down in history as one of the greatest – perhaps the very greatest ever – polo teams the world has known."

At Meadow Brook in 1930 the story was even gloomier for England. The scores were 10–5 and 14–9 in America's favour and the teams as follows: USA – Eric Pedley, E. A. S. Hopping, Thomas Hitchcock Jr, Winston Guest; England – Gerald Balding, Luis Lacey, Captain Pat Roark, Humphrey Guinness.

LEADERS OF THE U.S. POLO ASSOCIATION IN 1921: WILLIAM A. HAZARD (SECRETARY AND TREASURER) AND (*right*) H. L. HERBERT (CHAIRMAN). Hazard was secretary and treasurer from 1898 until his death in 1922

THE UNITED STATES TEAM AT MEADOW BROOK IN 1924. (*Left to right*) Devereux Milburn, Malcolm Stevenson, Tommy Hitchcock Jr and J. Watson Webb

MAJOR VIVIAN LOCKETT, CAPTAIN OF THE 17TH LANCERS TEAM, RECEIVING THE BADMINTON CUP FROM HRH THE DUKE OF GLOUCESTER AT RANELAGH IN 1922. The regiment defeated Cowdray Park in the final

WORCESTER PARK, 1923. Lord Wimborne with (*right*) Col. E. D. Miller, the polo writer

The American Captain, Eric Pedley, hailed from California though he was the son of a British Army officer. "Without doubt [he was] the finest Number 1 I have ever seen," said Hitchcock. "No one has equalled his performance versus England in 1930." For the England side, Pat Roark was an Irishman from an outstanding equestrian family. He learned his polo in India and soon showed a remarkable intuition for the game, a polo-sense which, coupled with stylish rhythm, speed and accuracy, put him in a bracket with his fellow Co Carlow player of the previous century, John Watson. Roark was the pivot of the 1930 English Westchester team.

1936

Knowing that the HPA would have difficulty in raising the money to send a team to the States in 1936, the Americans generously agreed to waive their right as holders of the Cup, to meet the British on their own ground. The contest was therefore played at Hurlingham in June, and for it the American selection committee brought in two more stars who eventually were to play off 10 handicaps. These were Stewart Iglehart, all-round athlete, scratch golfer and leading ice hockey player; and Mike Phipps, whose polo began at the age of 18, who formed a celebrated partnership with his lop-eared pony, Brown Fern, and who, it was said, had a rare gift for "appearing out of the blue". The Hurlingham selection committee (Colonel Fanshawe, Lord Kimberley and Colonel Ritson) chose Hesketh ("Hexie") Hughes, a product of the Rugby club, with much experience in the Argentine, to be England's Number One; Gerald Balding, now a

COWDRAY PARK, 1929. Lady Louis
Mountbatten and Capt. Pilkington Mullen

ROYAL BROTHERS IN THE SADDLE. HRH The Prince of Wales (afterwards King Edward VIII) and (*right*) HRH the Duke of York
(afterwards King George VI)

84

9-goaler, who had been playing a lot in the States, to be Two; Eric Tyrrell-Martin, a member of Major Magor's champion Panthers team, who had spent most of the last two seasons playing in California, at Three; and Captain Humphrey Guinness of the Royal Scots Greys, a champion rackets player, at Back, the position he held in the 1930 Westchester. (As previously mentioned, Rao Rajah Hanut Singh was invited to play, but a riding accident prevented him from doing so.) So the line-ups were as follows: USA – Eric Pedley (7), Mike Phipps (8), Stewart Iglehart (8), Winston F. C. Guest (8); England – Hesketh Hughes (7), Gerald Balding (9), Eric Tyrrell-Martin (8), Captain H. P. Guinness (7).

Of the 53 ponies which the Americans brought over with them, half were bred in the Argentine, half in the United States. The owners were Guest, Iglehart, Phipps and C. B. Wrightson (whose string was over with his team, the Texas Rangers). England drew on a stable of 47, of which 20 were bred in England and Ireland, 18 in the Argentine, 5 in Australia and one each in France, India, Spain and the United States. Among those who lent ponies for the English were: Lord Louis Mountbatten, Sir Harold Wernher, the Duke of Roxburghe, Major N. W. Leaf, Lord Cowdray, Major J. F. Harrison, Major Rex Benson, the Maharajah of Jaipur and Rao Rajah Hanut Singh. The British Master of Horse was Captain M. P. Ansell, of the 5th Royal Iniskilling Dragoon Guards. (Blinded in the Second World War, he later came to fame as Colonel Mike Ansell of the British Showjumping Association.) The Americans had the advantage, for the most part, of riding ponies they knew.

First American Lady Polo Player. "I don't like him to play against"
Second American Lady Polo Player. "Oh, why not?"
First American Lady Polo Player. "Well, he always plays as if I was only a woman."

The matches were played in seven chukkas each on June 10th and June 20th (the long interim being explained by a combination of rain and Royal Ascot). Although the Americans won both, their victories, 10–9 in the first and 8–6 in the second were much lighter than had been generally expected.

Everything was beautifully organized by the Hurlingham authorities. Nor would they allow interruptions. "A cluster of photographers followed the players," said one of their spokesmen, "but it had been arranged to dispense with the usual formality of photographs of the team before the match, and much to their disappointment and discomfiture, the camera-men were waved off the field." The band of the Duke of York's Royal Military School heralded the players, who came on accompanied by riders holding the Stars and Stripes and the Union Jack, and the crowd "rose in one body" as the two national anthems were played. In the Royal box with the Duke and Duchess of Gloucester were the Athlones, the Anthony Edens, Prince Arthur of Connaught and that great polo enthusiast, King Alfonso of Spain. Close by was the referee Mr Jack Nelson, chairman of the Argentine Polo Association. There was much betting, one of the heaviest wagers being that of Lord Castlerosse who bet £1,000 to £100 on the Americans (afterwards admitting that "I watched the polo with mixed emotions".)

> "It was one of the finest and most exciting games ever played," [said *The Times'* correspondent of the first match]. "There was little or nothing between the two teams from start to finish, and if anything England can count themselves unlucky to have lost. A slight superiority in pony power was responsible for the Americans' victory, although the English side very nearly negatived this disadvantage by their hard riding and dashing play . . . Mr Hughes gave the opposing Back, Mr Guest, no rest at all. . . . Mr Balding's hitting on both sides of his ponies was a marvel of accuracy. England's captain, Mr Tyrrell-Martin . . . covered his Back magnificently and started an attacking movement on every possible occasion. . . . Captain Guinness hardly made a mistake of any kind during the afternoon."

"Possibly the winners would have won more decisively had Mr Hitchcock been in their ranks", another observer opined, (Thomas Hitchcock Jr pleaded "pressure of business" in 1936), "but it was a side for America to be proud of." The *Morning Post* representative thought that "although Michael Phipps was beautifully mounted, he spoilt much of this advantage by faulty hitting. Iglehart was the best of the Americans, in that he kept his position however the game was running."

The close tussle of the first match proved so popular that its audience of 8,000 swelled to over 12,000 for the second "which easily constitutes a record for polo in this country," said a satisfied Hurlingham commentator. He continued:

> "In these happy circumstances the visit of our friends from the USA became an assured monetary success, which is just as it should be as the task of running these international matches is a most costly business. . . . There was no question of long odds on America this time." A racing man would have been correct in estimating them at about 5 to 4 on the visitors. There was little to choose between the teams. . . . In the last minute of the seventh chukka England had the ball almost on America's goal-line, within a foot of the opposite post. Then ensued one of the most exciting moments ever experienced by polo players or spectators. One player after another endeavoured to get in a hit at the stationary ball. The goal-post was knocked flat. A groan went up from the crowd when one

MRS HITCHCOCK, (MOTHER OF TOMMY HITCHCOCK JR AND CAPTAIN OF THE OLD AIKEN TEAM) AT STICK-AND-BALL. The man behind the party of sportswomen is Earl Hopping, who was in the 1930 American Westchester team

TROUVILLE, FRANCE, 1920. Baron Robert de Rothschild takes his stick

PRESENTATIONS. H.H. The Maharajah of Jaipur, captain of the Jaipur team, receiving the Ranelagh Open Challenge Cup from General Sir Bindon Blood, 1933. The present Maharajah stands with his brother to the right

of the defenders got in first smack and saved the situation for America. Had the ball gone over the line the score would have been seven goals all. Only one goal came in the final chukka and that was for the visitors who thus won by 8 goals to 6. . . . Mr Iglehart was the star performer of the day . . . Dismounting, the successful players went up to receive the Westchester Cup from the hands of the Duchess of Gloucester, and were heartily cheered by the thousands who had scampered to watch this pleasant ceremony.''

Will Ogilvie was then invited to take up his pen again:

The Westchester Cup

Here's to Guest *and* Iglehart!
Here's to Pedley! *Here's to* Phipps!
Each has filled a hero's part –
If they've torn our flag to strips,
Theirs in admiration dips

88

To the strenuous game we played
And the gallant fight we made
Ere accepting our eclipse.

Destined for their rich reward
These were foes to test our steel,
Mighty men before the Lord,
Wire and whipcord head to heel,
Sent their victories to seal
With one more triumphant ride
So that on the Other Side
Once again the bells might peal.

Here's to Guinness, Balding, Hughes,
Tyrrell-Martin! *– England's pride;*
"Bound," said everyone, to lose,
And to be beaten to the wide!"
Yet they raised a perfect ride,
Held them, ran them to a neck,
And, although they came to wreck,
None can fault the English side!

Not in life of living men
Shall such worthy rivals meet,
Shall such galloping again
Lead to victory and defeat.
Never shall the years repeat
Such a clash of East and West –
Polo at its splendid best;
Pluck and sportsmanship complete!

1939

Everything seemed to go wrong for the English challengers in the Westchester of 1939, which was played once again in the United States. They had hoped to supplement their string of ponies with some Argentine flyers, but, ahead of them, the Americans scooped the cream of the market. They had envisaged building the team around the 9-goaler Captain Roark but he died from injuries incurred in a fall during a practice match in February at Pasadena, just one month after the birth of a son to his American wife, Patsy Hostetter Smith, whom he had married in 1938. Major Bob Leaf, who had gone ahead with the ponies, fell ill and died, and Gerald Balding, the team captain, who already had quite enough to contend with, was obliged to take charge of the stables. Under the (non-playing) captaincy of Lord Cowdray, the British squad that crossed the Atlantic that spring was comprised of Tyrrell-Martin, Hughes, Balding, John Lakin, Aidan Roark (brother of Pat) and Bob Skene, who was qualified to wear the British colours as a Commonwealth (Australian) citizen.

THE FIRST AUSTRALIAN 10-GOALER: BOB SKEENE (IN 1938). He became a naturalized American

THE SKENE SADDLE. Devised by Bob's father, Curtis Skene, and made in Australia in 1939, it was described as "having a short, ample seat, with a high cantle . . . the flap cut rather straight with a small knee roll. . . . It helps keep the point of balance considerably further forward than is the case with the conventional English saddle. . . ."

GENERATIONS OF A CELEBRATED
AMERICAN POLO FAMILY.
Charles Armstrong and his son.
They are respectively, the
grandfather and father of the
well-known poloists Charles
and Stewart Armstrong

In the autumn of 1938, the U.S. Polo Association committee drew up an impressive
short list of 13 to defend the cup: Tommy Hitchcock (handicap 10), Stewart Iglehart
(10), Michael Phipps (10), Cecil Smith (10), Eric Pedley (8), Raymond Guest (8), William
Post II (8), Elmer Boeseke (7), Winston Guest (7), Ellbridge Gerry (7), Pete Bostwick (7),
Robert Gerry (6) and Cornelius Vanderbilt Whitney (6). Cecil Smith, a renowned Texan
horseman, who won many prizes in his youth for roping at the rodeos, started late in
polo. Having learned the rudiments from Rube Williams, he was introduced to
first-class polo by George Miller. Britain first saw him as a member of Wrightson's Texas
Rangers in 1936, but being unfit in the summer of 1939, his place was taken by Winston
Guest, who had played Back for America in 1930 and 1936. Son of an Englishman,
Captain the Hon. F. E. Guest, and grandson of the great polo patron, Lord Wimborne,
Winston Guest first played for the US national squad while still a Yale freshman. The
other positions were filled by Hitchcock, Phipps and Iglehart.

That very formidable combination won 11–7 and 9–3, thus keeping the Westchester
in America forever. For quite apart from the threatening war-clouds, England seemed
to have concluded she was irrevocably outmatched. A writer in the *Polo Monthly* of
August 1939 gave his opinion as to what was wrong with British polo:

"It is quite conceivable that by this time every polo player is heartily sick of the
words 'Westchester Cup', but the excuse for bringing it into this article, is that
recent events at Meadow Brook have made it clearer than ever that one of the
chief causes for our constant failure, perhaps the chief of all, is that no English
player has nowadays the skill to hit the ball as hard or as straight as do the
Americans. That cannot be attributed to lack of power for we, physically, are in
no sense the inferiors of our cherished enemies. Even if the international series
for that singularly ugly (but coveted) trophy came to an end last month perhaps
for all time it would still be worth while if we could improve our striking to
within reasonable distance of our recent opponents.

"Going back to first causes it will be admitted that the young American from
the age of 12 or thereabouts is taught and practised in the essentials of the game

UNITED STATES PLAYERS IN ENGLAND, 1936. (*Left to right*) Ellbridge T. Gerry, Eric Pedley, Stewart B. Iglehart, Robert E. Strawbridge Jr, Winston Guest and Michael G. Phipps

as none of us are. By the time they get into real polo, after an apprenticeship on bicycles, graduating to slow chukkas on experienced ponies, they know at least what they are trying to do and can devote themselves to the game whole-heartedly.

"Consider the case of the young Englishman also just beginning: he goes into slow polo with little idea of what it is all about and has to pick up what he knows in the hard school of trial and error to the objurgations of more experienced performers behind him (for our practice is always to put him up at No. 1, perhaps the most important position in the team), and what he learns he learns with twice as much labour and sadness as does his remote relation on the other side of the Atlantic.

"What is not generally conceded in England is that horsemanship in polo, though connected closely enough with the elements of riding as taught, is an art apart. Polo is a ball game and nothing else, though it is often mistaken for an equestrian exercise, and until that is fully realized by those whose delight it is to train the young player we shall continue to see faulty expositions of how the ball is struck until the end of time.

"Polo is a ball game and that means briefly that the same principles of striking the ball at rackets, for instance, obtain at polo. No ball game can be played sitting

92

FAMOUS AMERICAN PLAYERS OF THE INTER-WAR YEARS. (*Above left*) W. Holden White, (*above right*) Michael Phipps, (*below left*) Raymond and Winston Guest and (*below right*) Stewart Iglehart

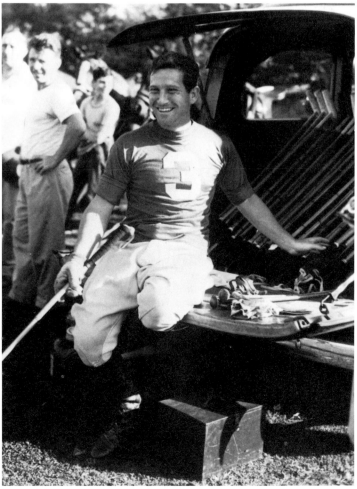

The Legend of the Ashton Brothers

Australian Polo Song

(To the air of The Campdown Races)

Eight bright ponies on a field of green
Polo! Polo!
A bright white ball that flies between;
And the music that we love,
Of galloping feet and the cheers that peal.
Polo! Polo!
And the racing colours, and the arms of steel,
And a windless blue above.

Chorus: *G'wine to dance all night,*
G'wine to ride all day
Polo week's but once a year.
Here's to the game we play!

A thoroughbred mare, with an Arab air,
Built for Polo!
14.3 and as keen as we
To follow the flying ball.
She loves the click of the swerving stick.
Polo! Polo!
And she'll bump her way where the scrum is thick,
And out and away from them all.

(Chorus)

Loud o'er the clatter the captains call
Polo! Polo!
"Ride your man!" or "Take the ball!"
Quickens the rattling pace.
All flat out as the goal draws near.
Polo! Polo!
But the cool-headed Back hits the ball out clear;
And way upfield you race.

(Chorus)

Then home on their station the ponies say
Polo! Polo!
"We don't mind work, if we have some play.
When the sheep tale slackens up."
And when they are old they'll teach the foals
Polo! Polo!
And show them how they scored the goals,
Playing at the Dudley Cup.

Anon

RIDING OFF. G. D. Armour

THE TEN-GOALER. Cecil Aldin

PONY LINES. G. D. Armour

CARPET BEATERS v. BOBBERY WALLAHS. **Snaffles**

HURLINGHAM. Gilbert Holiday

THE AUSTRALIAN ASHTON BROTHERS AS SEEN BY "THE TOUT"

101

Just as Indian polo was brightly illuminated, during the 1920s and '30s, by the name Hanut, so the game in Australia was to be dominated by a single name too: that of Ashton. But in contrast to the Rao Rajah's insistence that "there is only *one* Hanut!" there were no fewer than four Ashtons, tall, wiry, rugged brothers from New South Wales, who, by comparison with the well-heeled American, Argentinian and British players, came from a relatively impecunious background. Their self-made father, who left home at the age of 10 to take a job paying two shillings and sixpence a week, and then became a journalist and businessman, went on to spend 40 years in the NSW Parliament and was at one time acting State premier. The boy's mother, Helen, was the keen equestrian. She had already produced James Junior, Robert and Geoffrey when Phil arrived. "And now you have a polo team!" joked the doctor who helped deliver him.

The Ashtons were happily ensconced on the waterfront by Sydney harbour, until in the 1920s "J.A." bought a country house close to Goulburn, where a Colonel Macartney, who had played the game in India, had established a polo club, ostensibly for army officers, "as a bait to entice some young wartime men to stay in the service". When the Ashton boys told their father they were keen to start playing at Goulburn, he replied, "That's only for rich playboys." His wife did not agree. "Oh, come on," she said, "it'll be a good way of keeping the family together." James Ashton relented. "All right, if you take it up seriously and live within your means," he eventually agreed, "you can go ahead." That was around 1920 when Jim and Bob took up the game; in 1925 they were joined by Geoff and Phil, and from then until 1939, the brothers played as a team.

In fact Australian polo did not bear the plutocratic image it carried elsewhere in the world. It was a rural sporting tradition in which polo ponies were also stock horses for cattle and sheep graziers. And the Ashtons were sheep ranchers. Bob, the second oldest brother and family historian wrote this memoir in his diary about their first match:

THE ASHTON BROTHERS AS SEEN BY THE PHOTOGRAPHER. (*Left to right*) James, Robert, Geoffrey and Phil

"We had two ponies – Ray, a rough station horse, whom we bought with the place, and a little brown mare, about 20 years old, that had been played by John Garvin before the war. I took the two horses in on Friday – nearly 53 miles on rough road, which was a darn long ride. Jim had to supervise the shearing on the Saturday morning, so by the time he finished up and paid the shearers a cheque or two and got away it was after one o'clock. The old Dodge car had two punctures on the way in, so Jim didn't arrive until the fourth chukka. Of course, no one had ever played before and up to this time there was no score. Jim had had a game or two in Queensland and for some reason seemed able to hit the ball twice running. He also had the old polo pony. He proceeded to hit the first few goals and so made it look more like a game."

In the mid 1920s New South Wales polo was dominated by the Ross brothers, Knox, Bill and Tom, who with A. C. McLaurin, formed the Harden team. But by 1928, the Ashtons were taking over the lead. "Our strength," said Geoff Ashton, "was that, as a team, we lived together, talked together and always played together." Having become champions in their own country they were keen to make a name for themselves in the world at large. In 1929, saving up a good sum from the farm, they conceived the idea of shipping themselves and their ponies, quite independently, to play a season in England, with the ultimate ambition of winning the Hurlingham Championship Cup, then selling their ponies to pay for the expedition. The collective mind of sporting Australia boggled. 25 ponies in a small boat! The journey would take all of two months. How could they possibly stand the rigours of such a sea voyage? And, even if they did so, surely it would be six months after that before they were fit enough to play.

The boys would not be put off. They built experimental loose boxes; they had leather shoes made and tried the ponies out, thus shod, on wet slopes; and, when those failed, they made shoes of matting. Then they hired a little ship called *Port Huon* with wooden decking from bow to stern; and one January morning in 1930 they and their three grooms loaded her up with buckets, brooms, forks, baskets, rugs, lanterns, tools, nails, saddlery, matting, straw, luggage, sand for the exercise yard and a great deal of forage. Jim, Geoff and Phil went aboard; Bob, an atrocious sailor, followed in a liner with Mrs Ashton.

Seasick, the ponies were off their feed for the first few days and almost every day fresh problems arose. Each pony received a thorough daily exercise, which in itself was a simple matter. The hazard was in making the journey from the boxes – each pony being exercised separately – to the little sand-based exercise yard, a journey that had to be made 25 times a day. Then the malthoid roofs came loose, the exercise yard lost a high proportion of its sand in the wind, while one mare, Hilda, refused to leave her box, more often than not simply staring at the sea in acute alarm.

At about midnight one night in the Mediterranean a storm carried a wave over the port side of *Huon* damaging those aft boxes so severely that the occupants had to be moved to share with three others. Magic (a pony that would later fetch £4,000) got under a rail with her quarters overboard and was only retrieved after hours of heaving. By the time the storm was over, the brothers had half the ponies in pairs; and those that were doubled up, being unable to lie down, all too often kicked and fought. But there was little trouble after the Straits of Gibraltar. "We rolled quite heavily in the Bay of Biscay; but while we slid to the scuppers on the worst rolls, the horses showed no sign of trouble. Given good footholds on mats and room to sway about a horse can stand in rough weather without the slightest difficulty."

103

THE ASHTONS EXERCISING THEIR PONIES ON THE LITTLE BOAT THAT TOOK THEM
FROM AUSTRALIA TO ENGLAND IN 1935

They completed the 13,327 miles from Sydney to Hull in 48 days. After less than a week the ponies were fit to ride. Following a fortnight's stick-and-ball and practice games the Goulburn team were in a tournament. Within a month of that they were playing in the final of the Hurlingham Championship Cup. Although they did not win it, King Alfonso of Spain, who presented the prizes that year, was so impressed with both their adventure and play in the tournament that he arranged for another trophy to be awarded to old James Ashton. And as one newspaper reported: "The Ashton brothers, with their charm and tanned good looks have been an immediate social success." Geoff recalled that "a lot of English girls thought we were pastoral millionaires. Nothing, however, was further from the truth. Wool was down to ten pence a bale. We reckoned there was more money in polo ponies than sheep. . . ." But bad news was looming.

The economic depression having settled fairly and squarely on the world, more British players were disposing of their ponies than buying them. However, the brothers came in for a fresh turn of luck. American poloists, who had seen them in action, suggested through their national association, that the Goulburn team be invited over for a series of matches. Although the brothers were aware that they stood a far better chance of selling their ponies in New York State than in Britain, the expense of shipping them there would be almost more than they could stand. "We didn't have gambling temperaments," said Geoff, "but when we boarded the ship for New York I guess we made the biggest gamble of our lives."

Of the seven matches they played they only lost two and, what was more, all their ponies earned a fat price for them. To name one transaction, the tycoon, John Phipps, paid $5,000 for a dun mare called Checkers, which the brothers bought "for a song" from a backyard in Nowra, NSW, but was "the darling of the English press". Others, which had become household names in the British and American polo worlds, were bought "by such millionaires as Jock Whitney, Henry Talbot and Winston Guest".

With the depression deepening in Australia, James Ashton came in for some caustic comments about his sons' gallivanting "while the country suffered". But the Sydney critics were soon hushed into admiration when they saw the newspaper headlines after the auction in New York: "ASHTONS SELL PONIES IN U.S. FOR $77,000."

Having thus put Australian polo on the world map the brothers proceeded to win the New South Wales Championship Countess of Dudley Cup in 1934 and 1935. Bob and Phil Ashton, accompanied by 14 ponies and 2 grooms repeated the Sydney-Hull expedition in 1936. On that occasion they played for Major J. F. Harrison's team, The Knaves. In 1937 all four brothers made another successful English tour. With Bob Skene replacing Phil they won the Hurlingham Championship Cup which had just eluded them seven years before.

Indian twilight

Modern polo had thrived in India for over 70 years when the Second World War came. While many rajahs fielded private teams, the officers of each of the cavalry regiments stationed there had 500 troop horses – of a useful 15.0 or 15.3 hands – to choose from. India could count as many as four teams aggregating 28-goal handicaps or more, while five perennial high-goal handicapped tournaments were staged. The infantry battalions of the British Army in India each had a fair nucleus of service horses, too, and many of their officers played the game on their pay. By 1937, however, conditions were becoming more difficult. The Nazi menace was looming, mechanization rolled forward, everything was getting more expensive, while officers were required to work harder, play less.

Not only was polo in India eclipsed by a war, but its light was dimmed forever. Not long after Independence and the British departure, Congress dethroned the princes; thereafter the game was more or less confined to the slender horsed cavalry of the new national army with clubs only at Jaipur, Delhi and Calcutta (the first Calcutta Polo Club having been inaugurated in 1862).

But, for a last nostalgic look at polo in India under the British *Raj*, let us wind the clock back to the 1890s, and recall Kipling's image of the game. For polo gained its first literary classic in his story *The Maltese Cat*. It is an anthropomorphic tale of the inter-regimental final between the smart, expensively mounted Archangels and the Skidars ("what they call a Pioneer regiment"), the leading light of whose string of ponies is the "Cat" of the title. Here is my abridged version:

COLLISION AT QUETTA, 1939. Rissaldar-Major Ragbir Singh, of the Royal Deccan Horse, collides with the goal-posts — but scores!

The Maltese Cat

They had good reason to be proud, and better reason to be afraid, all twelve of them; for, though they had fought their way, game by game, up the teams entered for the polo tournament, they were meeting the Archangels that afternoon in the final match; and the Archangels' men were playing with half-a-dozen ponies apiece. As the game was divided into six quarters of eight minutes each, that meant a fresh pony after every halt. The Skidars' team, even supposing there were no accidents, could only supply one pony for every other change; and two to one is heavy odds. Again, as Shiraz, the grey Syrian pointed out, they were meeting the pink and pick of the polo ponies of Upper India; ponies that had cost from a thousand rupees each, while they themselves were a cheap lot, gathered often from country carts, by their masters who belonged to a poor but honest native infantry regiment.

"Money means pace and weight," said Shiraz, rubbing his black silk nose dolefully along his neat-fitting boot, "and by the maxims of the game as I know it — "

106

"Ah, but we aren't playing the maxims," said the Maltese Cat. "We're playing the game, and we've the great advantage of knowing the game. Just think a stride, Shiraz. We've pulled up from bottom to second place in two weeks against all those fellows on the ground here; and that's because we play with our heads as well as our feet."

"It makes me feel undersized and unhappy all the same," said Kittiwynk, a mouse-coloured mare with a red browband and the cleanest pair of legs that ever an aged pony owned. "They're twice our size. . . ."

Kittiwynk looked at the gathering and sighed. The hard, dusty Umballa polo-ground was lined with thousands of soldiers, black and white, not counting hundreds and hundreds of carriages and drags, and dog-carts, and ladies with brilliant-coloured parasols, and officers in uniform and out of it, and crowds of natives behind them; and orderlies on camels who had halted to watch the game, instead of carrying letters up and down the station, and native horse-dealers running about on thin-eared Biluchi mares, looking for a chance to sell a few first-class polo ponies. Then there were the ponies of thirty teams entered for the Upper India Free-For-All-Cup – nearly every pony of worth and dignity from Mhow to Peshawar, from Allahabad to Multan; prize ponies, Arabs, Syrian, Barb, country bred, Deccanee, Waziri and Kabul ponies of every colour and shape and temper that you could imagine. Some of them were in mat-roofed stables close to the polo-ground, but most were under saddle while their masters, who had been defeated in the earlier games, trotted in and out and told each other exactly how the game should be played.

It was a glorious sight, and the come-and-go of the quick hoofs, and the incessant salutations of ponies that had met before on other polo-grounds or racecourses, were enough to drive a four-footed thing wild.

But the Skidars' team were careful not to know their neighbours, though half the ponies on the ground were anxious to scrape acquaintance with the little fellows that had come from the North, and, so far, had swept the board.

"Let's see," said a soft, golden-coloured Arab, who had been playing very badly the day before, to the Maltese Cat, "didn't we meet in Abdul Rahman's stable in Bombay four seasons ago? I won the Paikpattan Cup next season, you may remember."

"Not me," said the Maltese Cat politely. "I was at Malta then, pulling a vegetable cart. I don't race, I play the game."

"O-oh!" said the Arab, cocking his tail and swaggering off.

"Keep yourselves to yourselves," said the Maltese Cat to his companions. "We don't want to rub noses with all those goose-rumped half-breeds of Upper India. When we've won this cup they'll give their shoes to know us."

"*We* shan't win the cup," said Shiraz. "How do you feel?"

"Stale as last night's feed when a musk-rat has run over it," said Polaris, a rather heavy-shouldered grey and the rest of the team agreed with him.

"The sooner you forget that the better," said the Maltese Cat cheerfully. "They've finished tiffin in the big tent. We shall be wanted now. If your saddles are not comfy, kick. If your bits aren't easy, rear, and let the 'saises' know whether your boots are tight."

Each pony had his 'sais', his groom who lived and ate and slept with the pony, and had betted a great deal more than he could afford on the result of the game. There was no chance of anything going wrong, and, to make sure each 'sais' was

107

shampooing the legs of his pony to the last minute. Behind the 'saises' sat as many of the Skidars' regiment as had leave to attend the match – about half the native officers, and a hundred or two dark, black-bearded men with the regimental pipers nervously fingering the big be-ribboned bagpipes. The Skidars were what they call a Pioneer regiment; and the bagpipes made the national music of half the men. The native officers held bundles of polo-sticks, long cane-handled mallets, and as the grandstand filled after lunch they arranged themselves by ones and twos at different points round the ground, so that if a stick were broken the player would not have far to ride for a new one. An impatient British cavalry band struck up "If you want to know the time, ask a p'leecman!" and the two umpires in light dust-coats danced out on two little excited ponies. The four players of the Archangels' team followed, and the sight of their beautiful mounts made Shiraz groan again.

"Wait till we know," said the Maltese Cat. "Two of 'em are playing in blinkers, and that means they can't see to get out of the way of their own side, or they *may* shy at the umpires' ponies. They've *all* got white web reins that are sure to stretch or slip."

"And," said Kittiwynk dancing to take the stiffness out of her, "they carry their whips in their hands instead of on their wrists. Hah!"

"True enough. No man can manage his stick and his reins and his whip that way," said the Maltese Cat. "I've fallen over every square yard of the Malta ground, and I would know." He quivered his little flea-bitten withers just to show how satisfied he felt; but his heart was not so light. Ever since he had drifted into India on a troopship, taken, with an old rifle, as part payment for a racing debt, the Maltese Cat had played and preached polo for the Skidars' team on the Skidars' stony polo-ground. Now a polo-pony is like a poet. If he is born with a love for the game he can be made. The Maltese Cat knew that bamboos grew solely in order that polo-balls might be turned from their roots, that grain was given to ponies to keep them in hard condition, and that ponies were shod to prevent them slipping on a turn. But, besides all these things, he knew every trick and device of the finest game of the world, and for two seasons he had been teaching the others all he knew or guessed.

"Remember," he said for the hundredth time as the riders came up, "we *must* play together, and you *must* play with your heads. Whatever happens, follow the ball. Who goes out first?"

Kittiwynk, Shiraz, Polaris and a short high little bay fellow with tremendous hocks and no withers worth speaking of (he was called Corks) were being girthed up, and the soldiers in the background stared with all their eyes.

"I want you men to keep quiet," said Lutyens, the captain of the team, "and especially *not* to blow your pipes."

"Not if we win, Captain Sahib?" asked a piper.

"If we win, you can do what you please," said Lutyens, with a smile, as he slipped the loop of his stick over his wrist, and wheeled to canter to his place. The Archangels' ponies were a little bit above themselves on account of the many-coloured crowd so close to the ground. Their riders were excellent players, but they were a team of crack players instead of a crack team; and that made all the difference in the world. They honestly meant to play together, but it is very hard for four men, each the best of the team he is picked from, to remember that in polo no brilliancy of hitting or riding makes up for playing

108

"THE SKIDARS WERE BEING GIRTHED UP . . ."

alone. Their captain shouted his orders to them by name, and it is a curious thing that if you call his name aloud in public after an Englishman you make him hot and fretty. Lutyens said nothing to his men because it had all been said before. He pulled up Shiraz for he was playing "back", to guard the goal. Powell on Polaris was half-back, and Macnamara and Hughes on Corks and Kittiwynk were forwards. The tough bamboo-root ball was put into the middle of the ground one hundred and fifty yards from the ends, and Hughes crossed sticks, heads-up with the captain of the Archangels, who saw fit to play forward, and that is a place from which you cannot easily control the team. The little click as the cane-shafts met was heard all over the ground, and then Hughes made some sort of quick wrist-stroke that just dribbled the ball a few yards. Kittiwynk knew that stroke of old, and followed as a cat follows a mouse. While the captain of the Archangels was wrenching his pony round Hughes struck with all his strength, and next instant Kittiwynk was away. Corks followed close behind her, their little feet pattering like rain-drops on glass.

"Pull out to the left," said Kittiwynk between her teeth, "it's coming our way, Corks."

The back and half-back of the Archangels were tearing down on her just as she was within reach of the ball. Hughes leaned forward with a loose rein, and cut it away to the left almost under Kittiwynk's feet, and it hopped and skipped off to

109

the Archangels' back to guard the goal; but immediately behind them were three Archangels racing for all they knew, and mixed up with them was Powell, sending Shikast along on what he felt was their last hope. It takes a very good man to stand up to the rush of seven crazy ponies in the last quarter of a cup game, when men are riding with their necks for sale, and the ponies are delirious. The Archangels' back missed his stroke, and pulled aside just in time to let the rush go by.

Bamboo and Who's Who shortened stride to give the Maltese Cat room, and Lutyens got the goal with a clean, smooth smacking stroke that was heard all over the field. But there was no stopping the ponies. They poured through the goal-posts in one mixed mob, winners and losers together, for the pace had been terrific. The Maltese Cat knew by experience what would happen, and, to save Lutyens, turned to the right with one last effort that strained a back-sinew beyond hope of repair. As he did so he heard the right-hand goal-post crack as a pony cannoned into it – crack, splinter and fall like a mast. It had been sawed three parts through in case of accidents, but it upset the pony nevertheless, and he blundered into another, who blundered into the left-hand post, and then there was confusion and dust and wood. Bamboo was lying on the ground, seeing stars; an Archangel pony rolled beside him, breathless and angry; Shikast had sat down dog-fashion to avoid falling over the others, and was sliding along on his little bobtail in a cloud of dust; and Powell was sitting on the ground, hammering with his stick and trying to cheer. All the others were shouting at the top of what was left of their voices, and the men who had been spilt were shouting too. As soon as the people saw no one was hurt, ten thousand native and English shouted and clapped and yelled, and before anyone could stop them the pipers of the Skidars broke on to the ground, with all the native officers and men behind them, and marched up and down, playing a wild northern tune called "Zakhme Bagān", and through the insolent blaring of the pipes, and the high-pitched native yells you could hear the Archangels' band hammering, "For they are all jolly good fellows", and then reproachfully to the losing team, "Ooh, Kafoozalum! Kahfoozalum! Kafoozalum!"

Besides all these things and many more, there was a Commander-in-Chief, and an Inspector-General of Cavalry, and the principal veterinary officer in all India, standing on the top of a regimental coach, yelling like school-boys; and brigadiers and colonels, and commissioners, and hundreds of pretty ladies joined the chorus. But the Maltese Cat stood with his head down, wondering how many legs were left to him; and Lutyens watched the men and ponies pick themselves out of the wreck of the two goal-posts, and he patted the Cat very tenderly.

"I say," said the captain of the Archangels, spitting a pebble out of his mouth, "will you take three thousand for that pony – as he stands?"

"No, thank you. I've an idea he's saved my life," said Lutyens, getting off and lying down at full length. Both teams were on the ground too, waving their boots in the air and coughing and drawing deep breaths, as the *saises* ran up to take away the ponies, and an officious water-carrier sprinkled the players with dirty water till they sat up.

"My Aunt!" said Powell, rubbing his back and looking at the stumps of the goal-posts, "that was a game!"

They played it over again, every stroke of it, that night at the big dinner, when

POLO PRACTICE.

MR. PUNCH'S HINTS TO BEGINNERS.

A 1920s SATIRE: *MR PUNCH'S HINTS FOR BEGINNERS.* G. D. Armour

LADY (WATCHING A PONY THAT HAS GOT UP AFTER A FALL). "Oh, he's all right, he's wagging his tail!"
G. D. Armour

AT A PRACTICE GAME. Groom: "Your pony, Sir!" Young novice (Somewhat shaken by a fall): "By Jove, yes – so it is. Thought I'd forgotten something!" G. D. Armour

PROVINCIAL POLO. He (watching the ineffectual efforts of the No. 1 to keep in the game). "You see, he's such a good supporter of the club we had to include him in the team." She: "Oh, I wondered. I thought it must be because he's so good-looking." G. D. Armour

POLO AND THE PUBLIC. Lady: "I wonder, 'Arry, how much the jockeys are paid for doing this?" Gentleman: "I dunno, but it would 'ave to be something pretty 'andsome if they wanted me to do it." G. D. Armour (Although this was doubtless most amusing in the 1920s, it now rings uncomfortably true!)

POLO AND THE PUBLIC. Lady spectator: "How dreadfully unfair. That one pushed the other just when he was going to hit the ball!" G. D. Armour

"AT ABOUT TWO IN THE MORNING . . . A WISE LITTLE, PLAIN LITTLE, GREY LITTLE HEAD LOOKED IN THROUGH THE OPEN DOOR"

the Free-for-All Cup was filled and passed down the table, and emptied and filled again, and everybody made most eloquent speeches. About two in the morning, when there might have been some singing, a wise little, plain little grey little head looked in through the open door.

"Hurrah! Bring him in!" said the Archangels; and his *sais*, who was very happy indeed, patted the Maltese Cat on the flank, and he limped in to the blaze of light and the glittering uniforms, looking for Lutyens. He was used to messes and men's bedrooms, and places where ponies are not usually encouraged, and in his youth had jumped on and off a mess-table for a bet. So he behaved himself very politely, and ate bread dipped in salt, and was petted all round the table, moving gingerly; and they drank his health, because he had done more to win the Cup than any man or horse on the ground.

That was glory and honour enough for the rest of his days, and the Maltese Cat did not complain much when his veterinary surgeon said that he would be no good for polo any more. When Lutyens married, his wife did not allow him to play, so he was forced to be umpire; and his pony on these occasions was a fleabitten grey with a neat polo-tail, lame all round, but desperately quick on his feet, and, as everybody knew, Past Pluperfect Prestissimo Player of the Game.

117

Chapter 6

YESTERDAY AND TODAY

Polo Wives, Polo Wives,
Theirs are dedicated lives
Spent in travelling far and wide
To cheer or criticise their side.
Polo wives, more nervous far
Than their playing husbands are
Like sentinels, spare sticks in hand,
Sit together in the stand.
"Look he's missed it!" "Oh the Brute!"
"Why not loft it like Hanut?"
"That's a cross, I do declare!
What no whistle? Tisn't fair!"
A broken stick! She quick must run
"Not that you fool, a fifty-one!"
Words may fly with tempers hot,
But polo wives don't care a lot.
The game is won, they all retire
for long post-mortems in the Bar.
But do not pity polo wives
Because they really love their lives.

Phyllis Critchley

Argentina the Mecca

Phyllis Critchley, wife of the pre-war 6-goaler Gerald Critchley, penned those lines during the 1950s when her husband was a regular player for Cowdray Park. As the mother of Major William Loyd, manager of the Guards Polo Club from 1973–85, she obviously speaks from the heart. Her verses make the game sound charmingly

118

ARGENTINES WHO WERE VICTORIOUS IN THE UNITED STATES IN 1954. (*Left to right*) Juan Nelson, Roberto Cavanagh, Luis Duggan, Manuel Andrada, Enrique Alberdi and Diego Cavanagh

amateur, and so it still is in most polo countries. And that includes the Argentine; for although the Argentinians play a more "professional" game than any other players in the world, there are no professionals in their country in the sense of players being paid for their services. Their proud poloists, while highly competitive by nature, play essentially for the sport, their "hired assassins" being found only abroad. Moreover, there is virtually no sponsorship in the Argentine.

Today Argentina boasts 150 clubs supporting more than 5,000 players thus rendering her – quite apart from her supremacy in terms of national team play – easily the most important polo country in the world. The vigorous grass roots of that nation's polo spring from her landowning element, nearly all of whom base their prosperity on beef cattle; for which, as we have seen, much the same handy horses are needed as the game requires. While the majority of the tournaments are played off at the clubs, much polo is played, too, at the *estancias*, the ranches.

It is often assumed by foreigners, because the major Argentine tournaments attract such enormous crowds, that polo there is a universal spectator sport, in the same way that football is elsewhere in the world (and indeed in South America itself). That is not exactly so. The crowds include a very high proportion of people who are more or less intimately connected with the players and their ponies: relations and close family friends, grooms and pony breeders.

Although Argentina took the Copa de las Americas from the United States in 1936, it was not until the Second World War – with which most of the other polo-playing countries were deeply preoccupied – that Buenos Aires became the acknowledged centre of the polo world. During the period 1943–44 alone, no fewer than five of her players were promoted to 10 handicaps: these were Enrique Alberdi, Luis Duggan, Carlos Menditeguy, Juan Carlos Alberdi and Julio Menditeguy. In the 1950s the name Roberto Cavanagh was added to the 10-goal roll; in the 1960s Horacio and Alberto Heguy, Francisco and Gaston Dorignac and Juan and Alfredo Harriot; in the 1970s Gonzalo Tanoira; and, in the 1980s, Daniele Gonzales and Gonzalo and Alfonso Pieres. In the last exhibition match in which two 40-goal teams competed, both Harriots, both Heguys, both Dorignacs, Tanoira and Gonzales were the gladiators.

America picks up the threads

While Argentine polo was in the ascendancy in the 1940s and North American polo was going into eclipse after Pearl Harbor, the United States suffered a major tragedy. On April 19th, 1944, Tommy Hitchcock Jr, by then a 44-year-old major commanding a fighter squadron in Britain, was killed when his P-51 crashed on Salisbury Plain on a training flight. America thus lost the man who should have been the leader of her polo in the post-war game. As it was, Elbridge Gerry, who was Chairman in Hitchcock's absence, handed over, in 1946, to Robert E. Strawbridge Jr, who made way in his turn, in 1950, to Devereux Milburn Jr.

By that time the land on which the Meadow Brook grounds lay had been requisitioned for highway development and, although the name survived in a successful team, the club was forced to close. The orientation of her national polo switched to New York and thence, under the leadership of Paul Butler, to Oak Brook, near Chicago. Texas, too, on the inspiration of the Barry family, became a great centre. Harold Barry (known to the Argentines as El Gordo, "the Fat One") held a 9-handicap for 15 years, his last appearance in the Cup of the Americas being in 1969, and in the US Open, alongside his son, Joe, with Hap Sharp's winning Tulsa-Greenhill team in 1970.

Argentina having won the Cup of the Americas on all six occasions since 1936, no further challenges were made after 1980. Meanwhile, Florida polo was expanding fast, and foreigners were beginning to identify the game in the United States in general with polo in that state. In the 1950s the Beveridge brothers, who took over the running of the Gulf Stream Club from Mike Phipps and Stewart Iglehart, started a fresh enterprise at Boca Raton, midway between Miami and Palm Beach.

In the early 1970s, William T. Ylvisaker, a prominent national player, (whose

THE MEXICAN BROTHERS WHO TOOK ON THE UNITED STATES IN 1946, DURING PRACTICE AT WESTBURY, LONG ISLAND. (*Left to right*) Gabriel, Guillermo (Memo), Alejandro and Jose Gracida. Memo Gracida is the father of today's celebrated Gracida brothers

THE GRACIDA BROTHERS AFTER COLLECTING PRIZES IN ENGLAND 14 YEARS LATER

THOMAS HITCHCOCK JR Believed by many pundits to be America's greatest-ever player, he was killed when his plane crashed on a training flight in Britain in 1944

brainchild is the Polo Training Foundation) began to establish the multi-million Palm Beach Polo and Country Club, which was to become the seat of the World Cup. Where polo features the market escalates and an inevitable and significant rise in property appreciation occurs. Billy Ylvisaker's club, like most American country clubs, caters for golf, croquet, swimming and tennis in grand style. But polo is – as he told me at the World Cup in 1985 – "my club's *raison d'être*". Extravagantly planted with palm trees and beds of exotic shrubs and flowers, the Club's 1,650 acres, which comprised poor ranchland until Mr Ylvisaker came along, now supports a massive jigsaw of luxury clubhouses and holiday lodges, 11 polo pitches, a magnificent grandstand and – because there are facilities for other equestrian activities, too – stabling for more than 2,000 horses.

By the 1980s the United States boasted more than 120 clubs, with over 2,000 names on its handicap lists, in addition to which nearly 2,000 tyros are involved in the game.

America's archipelago state of Hawaii has a long polo tradition. The game was started there by Louis von Tempsky in 1886 and enthusiastically taken up by the islands' cattle ranchers, grounds being laid over splendid sand bases at Honolulu and Maui. In 1913 a Hawaiian team brought home the coveted Bourn Cup from a final in San Francisco. In 1930 Walter Dillingham formed a celebrated family team with his three sons. In 1958 Fred Dailey, a real estate man, organized the Waikiki Club, and in 1965,

122

the Mokuleia Club, of which Mike Dailey is now in charge. Ronnie Tongg, a local attorney, who learned his game from such greats as Peter Perkins, Billy Linfoot and Bob Skene, became Hawaii's most prominent international player in the 1970s.

The Palm Beach World Cup

It was in 1978 that Palm Beach became the stage for the so-called "World Cup", which has been sponsored since 1983 by Piaget. When I flew out to cover the 1985 tournament of that name for *Country Life* and *The Times* a thunderstorm producing rain of monsoon proportions left the international pitch in such a state of flood that the finals had to be postponed. Next morning, which was a Sunday, three helicopters were brought in to fan the ground, and by three o'clock in the afternoon it was dry. A party of Marines carried on the Stars and Stripes, a vocalist marched in front of them and sang *God Bless America*, the spectators sat down as the words ended, girls with trays of popcorn and beer began to circulate in the plush crowded stadium and all was ready for the first chukka. In fact, the first match to be played was that for third place. The finals took place a week later.

The cup was won, 7–4, by White Birch Farm whose patron was America's most free-spending poloist, Peter Brant. He had the three Argentine Pieres brothers playing for him, Gonzalo (handicap 10), Alfonso (9) and Paul (6). I counted five out of White Birch's seven going to Gonzalo's unerring mallet. The opposing finalists were Geoffrey Kent's foursome, Rolex Abercrombie and Kent, who were completed by Antonio Herrera (9) of Mexico, Christian La Prida of Argentina (also 9 and afterwards declared

TEAMS RIDING TO THE PALM BEACH STADIUM BEFORE THE 1985 WORLD CUP

WILLIAM T. YLVISAKER, FOUNDER OF THE PALM BEACH POLO CLUB

''the most valuable player on the ground'') and Podger el-Effendi (8), who is by an Afghan father (serving in the Pakistan army) out of an Australian mother. The other team patrons were Helen Boehm (the Boehm team, previous World Cup winners), Alan Connell (Las Chachinas), William T. Ylvisaker (Concord) and Allan Scherer (Glenlivet Scotch). Boehm and Glenlivet competed for third place, which was secured by Glenlivet with superb coordination between Scherer's henchmen, Alan Kent (England), Stewart Mackenzie (New Zealand) and Alex Garrahan (Argentina).

In his foreword to the 1985 USPA handbook, the chairman, Summerfield K. Johnston Jr, wrote:

> ''In 1984, with the United States Polo Association only six years away from its 100th anniversary, polo in the United States has experienced an unprecedented growth. The majority of clubs all over the country, from the very smallest to the largest, have had an increase in playing members and have experienced overwhelming success in the staging of various tournaments, leagues and other club events. Corporate sponsors have become more and more interested in the sport and their participation as both team and tournament sponsors has helped promote polo at every level . . .

124

Activities and plans for the Polo Museum and Hall of Fame continue. Our continued efforts to market and utilize our marks and attract tournament sponsorships throughout Polo Properties produced somewhat of a mixed bag, but after a drawn-out and arduous legal battle, we feel we are at last in a position to begin to realize substantial benefits from this source. Funds derived from Polo Properties will initially be devoted to the very important task of improving our umpiring system and heightening the visibility and improving the caliber of our tournaments. . . .

On the international front, the newly formed International Federation of Polo [not recognized by the HPA] has become a functioning organization, and the prospect of a true world tournament in 1986 and 1987 appears to be a reality. . . . In April 1984 a team of young Americans travelled to Buenos Aires to participate in an international tournament and played at Palermo against two teams of young Argentine players. . . . The players who made this trip were Gene Fortugno, Bobby Barry, Owen Rinehart, Cali Garcia and Dale Smicklas.

Over the last four years under the leadership of Bill Sinclaire, much work has been done, and we can point with pride to the accomplishments of our committees, especially the Safety Committee which continues to monitor and attempt to improve the safety of the game both through the development of better equipment and better procedures and rules in matters directly affecting safety and security of our players. Special mention should also be made of the Umpire Committee, which is addressing the very difficult and challenging need for better umpiring by providing clinics and with a recently completed film.''

ALEX GARRAHAN AND ALLAN
SCHERER, OF GLENLIVET SCOTCH,
BY THE PALM BEACH
INTERNATIONAL GROUND

WHITE BIRCH: WINNERS OF THE 1985 WORLD CUP. (*Left to right*) Paul Pieres, Alfonso Pieres, Gonzalo Pieres and Peter Brant

Post-war revival in England

In 1945 the outlook seemed black for British polo. In 1939 the once glorious Hurlingham pitches were leased to Fulham Borough Council as allotments; and, in 1951, they were compulsorily acquired by the London County Council as public recreation grounds. Ranelagh suffered much the same fate; and, although Roehampton kept one ground open for the benefit of the Roehampton Open and the County tournament until as late as 1952, London polo, in its old pre-war guise, was dead. The Army had been the chief seedbed of British polo, and the old soldier players were not alone in predicting that the mechanization of the cavalry, coupled with short-term postings and longer parade hours, had dealt a desperate blow at the future of the game.

Yet, by 1946, polo was germinating quite strongly elsewhere in England. The Ham Club, which was founded in Richmond Park in 1926, was then revived by Billy Walsh and Cyril Harrison. At the same time, slow chukkas were being played at some of the county clubs, notably Rugby, Toulston, Taunton Vale, Rhinefield and Henley. Arthur Lucas established his Hertfordshire Club at Woolmers Park in the late 1940s, while the

Duke of Sutherland laid out a ground at Sutton Park, Guildford, and, in 1951 the Hon. Alistair Watson another in Suffolk. The Cheshire Club, which began in 1872, was revived in 1951, and the Cirencester Park Club, a foundation of the 7th Earl Bathurst in 1894 (and now Britain's third largest) was re-started by the present Earl and his brother, the Hon. George Bathurst, in 1952. The Kirklington Park Club, which began with Hugh Budgett in 1926 was resurrected by Alan Budgett in 1954.

"Rugby is thought to be the future headquarters of British Polo," John Board was writing in 1947. But the prophecy did not come true. Cowdray Park, in West Sussex, was the post-war springboard both of British international polo and of the game in England as a popular spectator sport. That mecca succeeded Hurlingham as the new "headquarters".

LEADING PERSONALITIES AT COWDRAY PARK BEFORE AND AFTER THE WAR: MR AND THE HON. MRS JOHN LAKIN. She is Lord Cowdray's youngest sister

A MATCH ON THE RIVER GROUND, COWDRAY PARK, IN THE 1930s

Lord Cowdray was largely instrumental in reviving English national polo in the post-war years; and he was easily the best qualified poloist to do it. His father (the 2nd Viscount, who had been Chairman of the HPA until he died in 1933) had laid out Cowdray Park's now famous House and River grounds a few years before the First World War, and the Lawns ground, under the old castle ruins, around 1930. Until the Second World War the Cowdray team played practice games on the Park grounds in April, then moved up to London to compete at Roehampton, Ranelagh and Hurlingham during the height of the season. They reverted to Cowdray Park for the Goodwood week tournaments, which were played off (as they are still) in late July and early August after the races.

In the early post-war years, the present Lord Cowdray not only possessed what must have been the largest stable of ponies in the country, a string of some 50, but he also hired them out at modest rates, thereby encouraging a number of young players – who probably later bought their own ponies. Conscious, too, of the need for polo recruiting from the Army, Lord Cowdray offered free chukkas on his club ponies to Sandhurst cadets.

He was fortunate to have retained the services of his stud groom, William Woodcock, who had been with him since his undergraduate days, in 1928, and who remained in the role until the late 1960s. Meanwhile that great horsemaster and equestrian, Harold Freeborn, was put on as master of horse to Lord Cowdray in 1950.

Lord Cowdray, himself a very useful player in the 1930s (a 4-goaler by 1939), might have gone far on the international scene during the post-war years, but for the loss of his left arm serving with the Surrey and Sussex Yeomanry in the British Expeditionary Force to France in 1940. Even so, clutching his reins with a hook and riding "confidential ponies", he continued to play regularly until the 1960s. In 1949 he captained the Cowdray Park team completed by three of his dedicated polo-playing

128

sisters, Mrs John Lakin, Mrs George Murray and Mrs Alistair Gibb. But his overall contribution to polo was much greater than individual examples can suggest.

During the summer of 1947 he got four three-a-side teams in action; and by the following season there were seven teams in the Goodwood week tournament. That year Jack Nelson and Luis Lacey came over from the Argentine with some ponies to watch the Cowdray polo. They were pleasantly surprised by the high standard of play they witnessed. They therefore invited Lord Cowdray to select and take a team to Buenos Aires in the autumn of 1949. The Argentine Polo Association (always readily conscious of the fact that it was the English who introduced the game to their country and who initiated their great pony-breeding industry) would not only host them, but also mount them throughout. Lord Cowdray took his brother-in-law, John Lakin, Lt-Col. Humphrey Guinness, John Traill Jr, Bob Skene and Lt-Col. Peter Dollar (who was almost back to his pre-war form, despite having been a prisoner-of-war for four years). They beat Chile, 12–9, and were only defeated 7–10 by the formidable Civiles. The teams were as follows: Chile – A. Chadwick, F. Astabaruga, P. Moreno, J. Lyon; Civiles – E. Lalor, A. Lalor, L. Lalor, J. C. Harriot. The British team having acquitted themselves very well, Lord Cowdray suggested a medium-goal return visit for 1951, and the Argentines were duly represented at Cowdray Park that year by La Españada – a 21-goal side composed of Buddy Ross, Luis Garrahan, Carlos (Laddy) Buchanan and Juan Reynal. The English team which beat them in three matches for the Coronation Cup included Lt-Col. Humphrey Guinness, Gerald Balding, John Lakin and Lt-Col. A. F. Harper, (since Hon. Secretary of the HPA).

In 1953, Coronation Year, over 12,000 people witnessed the international matches for the revived Coronation Cup at Cowdray Park. No such audience had attended an English tournament since the old Hurlingham days. The American team, Meadow Brook, was represented by Pete Bostwick, Philip Iglehart, Dicky Santamarina and Dev Milburn Jr; the Argentine by Ernesto Lalor, Alex Mihanovich, Juan Carlos Alberdi and Eduardo Braun-Mendez; England by Guinness, Balding, Lakin and Harper; and Chile by P. Moreno, F. Astaburaga, J. Zegers and G. Larrain.

Heading that crowd of over 12,000 people were Her Majesty the Queen (crowned on June 2) and the Duke of Edinburgh, who had started his polo in Malta in 1950 and now regularly wore Lord Cowdray's colours. Polo was once more a "Royal" game and there is no doubt that many who flocked to the matches at Midhurst went more in the hope of seeing the Queen and Prince Philip and Princess Margaret (several of whose friends played there) than to judge the finer points of the matches.

The Cowdray Park Gold Cup for the British Open Championship which began in 1956 remains the cordon bleu of English polo and the climax of the English season.

A potentially important new dimension was added to the game in that nation in the mid-1950s when Major Archie David – whose own club, Friar Park, at Henley-on-Thames, was attracting insufficient support – suggested the foundation of a new club based on the Household Brigade (the Household Cavalry and Brigade of Guards) at Windsor Great Park. The Duke of Edinburgh, Colonel of the Welsh Guards and by then a 5-goaler, welcomed the idea, consulted Lord Cowdray on the layout of grounds and secured the permission of the Queen, owner of the Park and Colonel-in-Chief of the seven regiments. Thus the Household Brigade – later renamed the Guards – Polo Club was established in 1955 – since becoming, with 10 playing pitches, the largest in Europe. The Queen's Cup, first presented by Her Majesty in 1960 is the club's premier high-goal tournament.

Of the 19 clubs in Britain two are in Scotland. The story of the game there goes back to

129

ARMY - NAVY MATCH - 5th May, 1954.

ROYAL NAVY - 4 Goals — ARMY - 2 Goals

ARMY v. NAVY, MALTA 1954. Lord Mountbatten and Col. Glover sit either side of the Queen, with Prince Philip on Col. Glover's left and Claude Burke(?) on Lord Mountbatten's right. (*Back row, left to right*) John Oram, Barrie Wilson, Robert de Pass and Pery Steindot

the 1890s when two horsed regiments were stationed at Redford Barracks, Edinburgh. There were also pitches for the Edinburgh Club at Murrayfield (long since the headquarters of Scottish rugby) and at Hopetoun. Aberdeen maintained a couple of polo fields too, and the highlight of the season was the tournament between the Edinburgh and Aberdeen clubs which was staged annually until 1934. That year, however, saw the departure of the cavalry on active service – never to return with their horses – and a long eclipse for the game.

Polo was brought back to Fife by the then factor to the Earl of Dundee, Captain

COWDRAY PARK TEAM, 1953. (*Left to right*) Lieut.-Col. Geoffrey Phipps Hornby, Viscount Cowdray, HRH the Duke of Edinburgh and Lieut.-Col. Peter Dollar

Mervyn Fox-Pitt, who learned the game at Sandhurst (in the days when Lord Cowdray gave free chukkas to the cadets); and continued playing during his service with the Welsh Guards. In 1981 Captain Fox-Pitt moved the club, by permission of the Earl of Mansfield, to the Scone Palace estate. Scotland's second club was established, in 1972, by John Douglas, Earl of Morton, on his Dalmahoy estate near Edinburgh. There is a strong tradition of polo in Lord Morton's family: his father and three Douglas uncles formed a family team between the wars. His own family team is composed of himself, his wife, his son James and his son-in-law, Richard Callander.

131

COWDRAY PARK, 1953. H.M. The Queen flanked by Viscount Cowdray and (*right*) The Hon. Mrs Robert Campbell Preston, Lord Cowdray's twin

England as an international centre

How would the international high-goal player like to spend his year, in terms of pleasurable variety and high-standard play? January and February might find him in Florida, at Palm Beach; the spring in Australia, New Zealand or possibly Spain; and then to England to prepare for that country's main championships in June and July. Mid-August might find him at Deauville and September back in England for the Guards Club's autumn tournament. And by late September or early October he would probably be in the Argentine where he would remain at least until the New Year.

I have posed the question: "What is your favourite polo country?" to players from a variety of nations, and the answer is almost invariably "England". Here is the reply given by the New Zealand 8-goaler Tony Devcich:

MORE WIT FROM THE 1920s: *IF POLO REALLY BECAME POPULAR.*
Supporter of Home Team: "Nah then, 'Urlingham, let's 'ave
one!" J. H. Dowd

AND YET MORE: "I've never seen a polo match before and I'm
dying to see the dear ponies kick the ball about."

THE GOULBURN TEAM. H. F. Bauer

SMITH'S LAWN, 1967. Joan Wanklyn

PONY LINES, CIRENCESTER, 1972. Terence Cuneo

◁ *Yesterday and Today* ▷

"I think the No 1 ground of the Guards Polo Club is the best I have ever played on. What's so good about England is that you have a season with tournament after tournament and all within easy striking distance of each other. Whether you are based at Windsor or Cowdray there is only a short distance to travel to get to the ground and there is play during the week as well as at weekends. But if you go to America and play there you sometimes have to travel 600 miles to the next tournament. Also in America many clubs just have club members playing for cups. Yes, England is the place . . . it is far more competitive."

FAMILIAR FIGURES ON THE POLO GROUNDS OF ENGLAND AS WELL AS INDIA: THE MAHARAJAH AND MAHARANEE OF JAIPUR. The photograph was taken on the occasion of the Maharanee's candidacy for the Swatantra Party in the 1962 Indian general election

THE UNITED STATES TEAM THAT CONTESTED THE CORONATION CUP IN 1953. (*Left to right*) Devereux Milburn Jr, Robert Santamarina, Philip Iglehart and Pete Bostwick

BICYCLE POLO AT SMITH'S LAWN, WINDSOR, 1967. HRH The Duke of Edinburgh and (*right*) the Australian poloist, Sinclair Hill

With high-goal, as well as medium- and low-goal tournaments at three of her clubs (Windsor, Cowdray and Cirencester), all in beautiful settings, England might well be regarded as the world's polo mecca, although the recession has hit the game there almost as badly as anywhere. Gone are the days when John Oxley could load 30 ponies into a Super DC8 and fly them into Heathrow in six hours. The price became prohibitive in the 1970s.

Every member of Oxley's stable was either the progeny or the grand-progeny of Woody Dee, the Walt Disney star, who died aged 28, in 1970. Oxley's son, Jack, played alongside him in the Boca Raton team, together with 240-lb Joe Barry and Oxley's master of horse Joe Casey, a (naturally) left-handed man who was positioned at One and who had broken and made every one of the 30 ponies. In 1970, largely owing to that pony power, they defeated formidable Windsor Park (Paul Withers, Pedro Gallardo, Lord Waterford and Lord Patrick Beresford), 13–10, in the final of the tournament for the Cowdray Park Gold Cup.

A number of other American poloists used to fly their teams and ponies to England. Next in fame were the Columbia foursome consisting of the veterinarian, Billy Linfoot, and his son, Corky, Heath Manning and the Hawaiian Ronnie Tongg; and Hap Sharp's Greenhill Farm with his son-in-law, Tommy Wayman and Harold (Chico) and Joe Barry.

The HPA International Day

Although England, in 1971, could still not field a national team worthy of taking on America's top four (and thus propose a Westchester revival), the Hurlingham Polo Association, then capable of mustering a 23-goal team, invited the Americans playing in England that year to compete for the Coronation Cup, which had originally been inaugurated as a national prize by the Ranelagh Club in 1910. The first poloists to have the honour of representing England in the new Coronation series were Paul Withers, the brothers Julian and Howard Hipwood and the Hon. Mark Vestey. The Americans were Tommy Wayman of Oklahoma, Billy Linfoot of California, William T. Ylvisaker of Illinois, and Chico Barry of Texas. The United States won 9–6 that year. With Corky Linfoot and Roy Barry in place of Ylvisaker and Wayman, they were on top 6–3 in 1972, (when, in England I, Ronald Ferguson replaced Vestey), 7–6 in 1973, and 4–3 in 1974. Major Ferguson, deputy chairman of the Guards Polo Club, has been the chief organizer of International Day from the beginning. He is to be warmly congratulated, not only for finding such generous sponsors as Wills, then the Imperial Group, then Cartier, and for making the programme function like clockwork; but also (with bands from the Brigade of Guards and trumpeters and drummers from the Household Cavalry) for adding a wonderfully glamorous spirit to the entire afternoon.

In 1975 when the Americans decided they could no longer afford to fly ponies to Britain and field a suitable representative team, the HPA invited the Argentines then playing in Britain to form a 27-goal squad for the Coronation Cup. This turned out to be Juan Jose Alberdi, who was pivot man to Eric Moller's Jersey Lilies that season, Eduardo Moore and Hector Barrantes, the Stowell-Foxcote duo, and Gonzalo Pieres. At the time, Pieres was a 19-year old student playing off a 3-handicap; he went on to become a 10-goaler earning a $1m team contract in the U.S.A. England was again beaten (10–6) and continued to suffer defeat annually until in 1979, she beat Mexico, 9–7. In 1982, England met a 28-goal New Zealand team deploying Stewart Mackenzie

1963 : SMITH'S LAWN, WINDSOR. Princess Anne holds her father's pony while he settles in the saddle to represent Windsor Park against Major Archie David's Friar Park

and John Walker – both sons of farmers who represented New Zealand in the 1950s and '60s – Cody Forsyth and Tony Devcich. This time, in the English team, the Hipwoods were joined by Alan Kent, who first started playing at Millfield School and in the New Forest branch of the Pony Club. Kent is a very fast forward who bought some excellent Jersey Lilies ponies after Eric Moller disbanded the team; and Lord Charles Beresford, the son of Ireland's leading player, the Marquess of Waterford and at 19 winner of the Best Young Player award in 1979. England won, 6–4.

England beat New Zealand again in 1983. In 1984 (when Howard Hipwood drew level with his brother Julian on the 9 handicap level), the English squad aggregate stood at 32, a post-war record. But they were just overwhelmed by a 31-goal cosmopolitan quartet ("The Rest of the World") comprised of Carlos Gracida (Mexico), Silvio Novaes (Brazil), Owen Rinehart (United States) and Cody Forsyth (New Zealand). Originally the pupil of that great stylist, Tommy Wayman, Rinehart, who was promoted (in England) to 9 goals in 1985, has been a brilliant pivot to David Jamison's and David Yeoman's champion team, Southfield. In 1985, when the English team was made up of the Hipwoods, Kent and Patrick Churchward (a veterinarian who manages the Sussex stud), Mexico was once more the opponent. The Mexicans were Memo Gracida (handicap 10) and his brother Carlos (9), their cousin Reuben (7) and Jesus Baez (5). The

1967: ROYAL PRIZE-GIVING AT WINDSOR. HM The Queen presenting the Westbury Cup to the Duke of Edinburgh. Prince Charles, who played Number One in Prince Philip's team, the Rangers, awaits his turn for a silver ash-tray

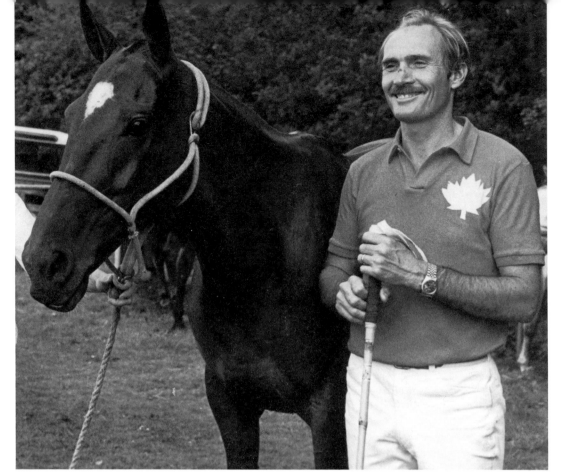

1985 COWDRAY PARK GOLD CUP PRIZE WINNERS. Galen Weston's champion pony, Abba, with Julian Hipwood who rode it with the victorious Maple Leafs throughout the tournament. Abba, a New Zealand pony, was broken and schooled by the New Zealander, Tony Devcich

where polo is on the extra-mural curriculum – and while there she was selected for the British junior fencing team. Going on to study agricultural economics at Oxford, it was not long before she was awarded a squash blue and a fencing half-blue.

When she was told that the University polo club was short of players, childhood memories came flooding back; and despite her parents' caution, the temptation to learn the game that combined horses with ball-play was overwhelming. Her first encounter was against Cambridge. Oxford won the match and she won her half-blue.

With an honours degree and a university travelling award she took a job, in her intellectual field, in Buenos Aires. Her brother, John, having succeeded her father as the mainstay of Woolmers Park, asked her to help him find horses. In the process, she not only learnt a lot about the breeding, making and care of polo ponies, but also, in Argentina's main polo centre, improved out of recognition her knowledge of the game.

The strength in a woman's arm can rarely, if ever, be that of a man's. But, given her games sense and outstanding coordination of limb and eye, it was not difficult for her to make up for that limitation through the acquisition of a fluent style and mastery of the perfectly timed stroke.

In 1967 she was playing polo with a young cavalry officer, one goal ahead of her on handicap, named Simon Tomlinson. Enrolling a couple of friends they formed a team which they called Los Locos.

In 1968 Simon and Claire married. Their polo went from strength to strength; their mutually supporting partnership in Los Locos forward positions soon became a byword, and so did their talent for recruiting the balance of their team from players who were most closely in harmony with them. Los Locos carried off nearly all the English low-goal trophies and in 1977 they won the principal medium-goal prize: Cirencester Park's coveted County Cup.

Simon and Claire live with their three children at Down Farm in Gloucestershire, a property that was occupied throughout the 1930s by the Beaufort Polo Club, whose membership included such illustrious sporting names as the Maharajahs of Jaipur, Jodhpur and Ratlam, Rao Rajah Hanut Singh, Humphrey Guinness and Gerald Balding. There a magnificent stables complex was built, with, above it, accommodation for the grooms, the whole establishment being run by the English high-goaler, Vivian Lockett.

Unless the polo player rides first-class ponies, which have been properly schooled and which he understands really well, he will never improve – as many of us know to our cost. The crowning satisfaction for the accomplished player is to breed his own "quality", to make the ponies which carry him to victory. The Tomlinsons' ponies were getting better and better (more than half their string are now home-bred) and, by 1978, by virtue of that, they were ready for the high-goal scene. (In Britain that means tournaments open to teams whose aggregate handicap is between 17-22 goals.)

When the Hurlingham Polo Association reminded them of the rule against women playing in high-goal matches, Claire Tomlinson, who was then handicap 3 and had played with 25-goal teams in Argentina, wanted to know why Britain should be the only country in the world with such an illogical stricture. The association remained adamant. Mrs Tomlinson and the other leading British woman player, Lavinia Black, organized a petition proposing that either they should be allowed to take part or their handicaps should be reduced below the recognized high-goal standard. The association relented.

In 1979 Los Locos – the Tomlinsons with their friends David Gemmell at Back and the long-hitting Argentine, Hector Crotto, in the pivot position – won the Queen's Cup at

141

1985 COWDRAY PARK GOLD CUP. HRH THE PRINCE OF WALES, OF LES DIABLES BLEUS, WITH THE PRINCESS, WHO PRESENTED THE PRIZES

PLAY BEFORE THE ROYAL BOX FOR THE 1985 CORONATION CUP AT SMITH'S LAWN, WINDSOR. The players (*left to right*) are Julian Hipwood (in possession for England I), Reuben Gracida and Carlos Gracida (Mexico), Howard Hipwood and Alan Kent (England I). Mexico won, 8–6

IN THE PONY LINES

Windsor Great Park from an entry of 12 teams, and, for the first time in the history of high goal polo, the Queen received a curtsey, instead of a bow, from the team member who stepped forward to receive the cup.

Two weeks later, Los Locos reached the final of the Cirencester Club's high-goal Warwickshire Cup tournament, from a field of 14, and they lost by as little as half a goal. By 1980, Claire was playing off a 4 handicap, the same as her husband. Claire Tomlinson knows just how to employ both her pony's impulsion and weight and her own to the maximum advantage. She is a woman who combines outstanding athletic ability with immense courage, determination and the will to win.

The Argentines in English polo

The Argentines, in terms both of gladiators and ponies, provided much of the backbone of English high-goal polo up to 1981. But no Argentine player has ridden onto English grounds since the outbreak of hostilities between the two countries. Until 1982 the list of those who helped form the main strength of the British teams was a long one, starting with Juan Jose Diaz Alberdi, Ricardo Diaz, Juan Cavanagh, Enrique and Juan Alberdi, Carlos Menditeguy, Alex Mihanovich, Gaston Dorignac, Negro Torres Zavaleta, Tito Lalor, Negro Goti, Celestino Garros; and continuing with Daniele Gonzalez, the Number Three of Lord Brecknock's triumphant Pimms, and Eduardo

CLAIRE TOMLINSON, THE WORLD'S TOP WOMAN PLAYER, WITH HER PONY, QUEENIE

are the vice-chairman and five committee members of the Guards Club.

"It does sometimes look like a world of galloping majors even if, statistically, the majority is a minority. It is slightly odd to find this type of person so involved in commercial sponsorship and so susceptible to wealth – old and new. One major, who did not want to be identified, said he thought there were a lot of very bad hats in the polo world. The word he used and which stuck in my mind was 'spoiled' and the implication, quite clear, was that there were some in the polo world who had more money than was good for them. Conversely there are those who think that elements of the polo establishment are behind the times and stuffy.

"The question of money irks many polo players, especially those who do not have a great deal of it (relatively speaking!) but those who are automatically regarded as millionaires just because they happen to play the game."

CHAMPION GIRLS TEAM, THE "FOUR GRACES". (*Left to right*) Jane, Pippa, Victoria and Katie. Their father, Peter Grace of New Zealand, runs the Rangitiki Polo School at Windsor

CORONATION CUP, 1979. Susie Whitcomb

NEIL CAWTHORNE DEPICTS PRINCE CHARLES IN POSSESSION OF THE BALL AT WINDSOR IN *THE LAST CHUKKA, 1981*

FULL TILT. Heather St Clair Davis

◁ *Yesterday and Today* ▷

The correspondent reporting from Lagos for *The Times* of February 2nd, 1981, while also highlighting the ostentatious reputation, reminds us, too, of modern polo's Anglo-Indian heritage:

"It was champagne and cigars at the Lagos Polo Club this weekend. . . . Polo is the game of the northern Hausa Muslim élite. In Nigeria, it is also the special preserve of army generals and royal emirs. Consequently, polo is the most hated symbol of northern dominance in the eyes of the western Yoruba. . . . Military police, resplendent in crisp white cravats, bright red caps and stiffly starched khaki, escorted guests to sofas set on carpeted lawns under gaily coloured marquees. Stewards bearing polo club crests passed drinks, while the 'old boys' settled to watch the chukkas. . . . The spectacle was more social than sporting. Rich northern *Agbadas* mixed freely with the trilbys and tweeds, bright cocktail dresses flashed through expensive leather boots and army crests. An end-of-tournament dinner dance was held on Saturday night with a barbecue and regimental bands on the lawns; members only and compulsory black tie. . . . The coveted gold cup was a gift from a rich northern businessman Usman Dantata. He too was playing, and boasted the highest handicap, and 48 of the horses on the field were owned by him. . . . Nigerian army officers are very pukka about their polo. The 'ungentlemanly' American-style helmet was not to be seen. The horses were beautiful thoroughbreds – preferably Arab ponies, otherwise Argentine. . . . When the day was done, as the orange glow faded upon a surging mass of spectators and players, glinting over the polished silver trophies, while the chief guest handed out the prizes, my host leant across his chair and said to me with unmistakable old Raj aplomb: 'Fine game. That last chukka was jolly good. Calls for a decent scotch, don't you think, old boy?'"

What so many casual spectators at the big cosmopolitan tournaments, dazzled by the superficial trappings of the event, often fail to appreciate, is the extraordinary dedication that goes into the game. Not only is immense stamina required of the players, but they must put in hours and years of practice before they become the accomplished performers that they are, and much thought and preparation are expended into welding their teams together. All this is to be very much admired, as is the courage, skill and physical fitness of their ponies, seen sleek and glittering in their patrons' colours in the lines; the habitual high standards of umpiring; and the pride that goes into the setting, the immaculately kept grounds, the pageantry and the nations' flags fluttering behind the spectators' stands. In any case, the fact that polo is an esoteric pursuit does not prevent it being magnificent spectator entertainment, even to the uninitiated. Above all, there is in polo a powerful tradition of honourable dealings and generous sportsmanship. All these things combine to help polo live up to its true image, as spelled out in the words of that time-honoured exhortation:

"Let other people play at other things,
The King of Games is still the Game of Kings!"

For the daring turn and the skilful stroke
The ever-quickening stride,
The ring of the stirrup, the clash of the stick,
And the rush of the furious ride;
The cheer when the ball through the goal is driven
By the steady hand and eye,
Have a wild delight in themselves alone
That can never grow old or die.

H. C. Bentley

BIBLIOGRAPHY

ARMOUR, G. D. *Bridle and Brush*. Eyre and Spottiswoode, 1937. Contains the artist's graphic accounts and drawings for *Country Life* of the 1913 Westchester series in the United States.

BENT, Newell. *American Polo*. Macmillan, 1929. A comprehensive history up to the late 1920s.

BOARD, John. *Polo*. Faber, 1956. A survey of the game with excellent drawings by the author.

BROWN, Paul. *Polo*. Charles Scribners' Sons, New York, 1949. Foreword by Robert E. Strawbridge, Jr. Brief instructional book with many drawings by the author.

BROWN, Paul. *Hits and Misses*. Derrydale Press, 1935. Beautifully illustrated by the author.

CHURCHILL, Winston S. *My Early Life*. Macmillan, 1930. Contained his pen-portrait of the priority given to regimental polo in India at the turn of the century.

CULLUM, Grover. *Selection and Training of the Polo Pony*. Charles Scribners' Sons, New York, 1934. With comments on the game.

DALE, T. F. *Polo: Past and Present*. Country Life, 1905. A good account of polo's early years by a sportsman who learned the game in India in the 1880s. Dale was "Stoneclink" of *The Field*.

DALE, T. F. *The Game of Polo*. Constable, 1897.

DALE, T. F. *Polo at Home and Abroad*. Country Life, 1910.

DAWNAY, Major Hugh. *Polo Vision*. J. A. Allen, 1984. The science of the game and how to learn and adopt it, by the proprietor of the Whitfield Court School, Co. Waterford.

DE LISLE, General Sir Beauvoir. *Tournament Polo*. Eyre and Spottiswoode, 1938. With illustrations by Maurice Tulloch.

DEVEREUX, W. B. Jr. *Position and Team Play in Polo*. Brooks Bros, New York, 1914.

DRYBROUGH, T. B. *Polo*. Vinton, 1898. Drybrough was captain of the Edinburgh Club team.

FORBES, Allan. *Sport in Norfolk County*. Houghton Mifflin, 1938. Descriptions of American provincial polo, sailing and hunting in the early years of the 20th century.

FORBES, William Cameron. *As to Polo*. George H. Ellis, Boston, 1918. A full description of the game.

◁ Bibliography ▷

GANNON, Brigadier Jack. *Before the Colours Fade*. Brief autobiography by the manager and secretary of the Hurlingham Club in the 1930s, who was well known in the post-war years for his articles in *The Field* and *Horse and Hound*. Contains a first-hand account of the 1936 Olympics.

GEERY, Addison. *Mallet and Hounds*. Privately printed, New York, 1931.

HATCH, Alder and KEENE, Foxhall. *Full Tilt: the Sporting Memoirs of Foxhall Keene*. Derrydale Press, New York, 1938. Limited edition of 950 copies.

HOBSON, Richard. *Polo and Ponies*. J. A. Allen, 1976. 45-page pamphlet.

HURLINGHAM POLO ASSOCIATION. Year Books.

KENDAL, Paul G. *Polo Ponies: Their Training and Schooling*. Derrydale Press, New York, 1933.

KIMBERLEY, Earl of (Ed.) *Polo*. (Lonsdale Library, Vol XXI). Seeley Service, 1930. With contributions by Brig.-Gen. G. Beresford, Major-General Geoffrey Brooke, Lt-Col. (later Brig.) Jack Gannon, "Marco", Brig-Gen. R. L. Ricketts and P. Vischer.

KIPLING, Rudyard. *The Maltese Cat*. Macmillan, 1898. The author's classic with a polo pony hero, in the 1890s. Included in his collection entitled *The Day's Work*. Macmillan produced a special edition, in 1955, with illustrations by Lionel Edwards.

LITTLE, K. M. *Polo in New Zealand*. Whitcomb and Tombs, 1956. A comprehensive account of the history of New Zealand polo and that of each of its clubs, 1889–1955.

LORD, John. *The Maharajahs*. Hutchinson, 1972. Contains references to the game, both in the Mogul days and in modern times.

LOVER OF THE GAME, A. *Letters on Polo in India: Written by a Beginner*. Thacker, Spink, Calcutta, 1918.

"LUCIFER". *Station Polo*. Thacker, Spink, Calcutta, 1896.

"MARCO". *An Introduction to Polo*. Country Life, 1931. Lord Mountbatten's classic, which went into five subsequent editions.

McGRATH, Sandra. *How the Mighty Ashton Brothers Rode into Sporting History*. Article in the Weekend Australian magazine, July 9–10, 1983.

MACMASTER, J. E. *The Mutt. (The Story of a Polo Pony)* Caxton, Idaho, 1955. Illustrations by Richard F. Ford.

McMASTER, Major R. K. (U.S. Army). *Polo for Beginners and Spectators*. Exposition, New York, 1954.

MELVILL, Col. T. P. *Ponies and Women*. Jarrolds, 1933.

MILLER, E. D. *Modern Polo*. Hurst and Blackett, 1902. Includes an interesting survey of pony breeds by one of the most authoritative makers and schoolers of ponies of his day.

MILLER, E. D. *Fifty Years of Sport*. Includes a strong polo section. Hurst and Blackett, 1925.

MORAY BROWN, J. *Polo*. Section on the game in the Badminton Library *Riding* volume. Longmans Green, 1891. Moray Brown was the most prominent polo correspondent on the early years of the game. Published separately in a 1896 edition with illustrations by Cuthbert Bradley.

NELSON, Juan D. and others. *El Polo en Argentina*. Explains vividly how, from modest beginnings the Argentine grew to be world's supreme polo nation.

PEARCE, Captain James J. *Everybody's Polo*. Robert Hale, 1949. A brief book concerning the author's experiences in a variety of countries.

POLO MONTHLY, 1921–39. These well illustrated magazines comprise a most useful documentary, from the British viewpoint, of the game between the two world wars.

RICKETTS, Brig.-Gen. R. L. *First Class Polo and Match Play*, (Gale and Polden, 1928).

◁ *Bibliography* ▷

ROLEX of Geneva. *World Guide to Polo Clubs*. Contains the addresses of nearly all the clubs and the facilities and officials' names in all the major clubs.

SPENCER, Herbert. *Chakkar: Polo Around the World*: Published in the 1970s by Drake and H. Spencer. A large book, with essays by a number of prominent players and very lavishly illustrated with colour photographs.

TRENCH, Charles Chenevix. *The Frontier Scouts*. Eyre & Spottiswoode, 1985. Contains an account of the 20th-century survival of the old Manipuri game.

UNITED STATES POLO ASSOCIATION. Year Books.

VICKERS, Lt-Gen. W. G. *Practical Polo*. J. A. Allen, 1958. A simple guide for beginners, illustrated, demonstratively, with "stick" men and "stick" ponies.

WATSON, J. N. P. *Country Life* articles. Including illustrated accounts of nearly all the British high-goal tournaments and many others, too, since 1970.

WHITE, Captain Wesley J. *Guide for Polo Umpires*. USPA, 1935. This small 77-page book went into six editions.

POLO CLUBS

Great Britain and Eire

ALL IRELAND POLO CLUB
Phoenix Park, Dublin

ANGLESEY POLO CLUB
Henblas, Bodorgan; also Anglesey Show
Ground, Mona

CAMBRIDGE UNIVERSITY POLO CLUB
Rutland Club, Oakham, Leicestershire

CHESHIRE POLO CLUB
Oulton Grounds, Little Budworth

CIRENCESTER PARK POLO CLUB
Cirencester Park, Gloucestershire

COLCHESTER GARRISON POLO CLUB
Ypres Road, Colchester Garrison, Essex

COWDRAY PARK POLO CLUB
Cowdray Park, Midhurst, Sussex

CYPRUS POLO ASSOCIATION
British Forces Cyprus, c/o Episkopi Polo Club

DUNDEE AND PERTH POLO CLUB
Birkhill Estate, Cupar, Fife; also Scone Palace
Polo Ground

EDINBURGH POLO CLUB
Dalmahoy Park, Midlothian

GUARDS POLO CLUB
Smith's Lawn, Windsor Great Park

HAM POLO CLUB
Ham House, Petersham, Surrey; also Richmond Park

KIRTLINGTON PARK POLO CLUB
Kirtlington Park, Oxfordshire

MILLFIELD SCHOOL POLO CLUB
Millfield School, Street, Somerset

OXFORD UNIVERSITY POLO CLUB
Kirtlington Park, Oxfordshire

RHINE ARMY POLO ASSOCIATION
Bad Lippspringe, West Germany

RHINEFIELD (NEW FOREST) POLO
CLUB
New Park Farm, Brockenhurst, Hants

ROYAL COUNTY OF BERKSHIRE
POLO CLUB
Windsor

ROYAL NAVAL EQUESTRIAN
ASSOCIATION
c/o Taunton Vale Polo Club

RUTLAND POLO CLUB
Rutland Show Ground

SILVER LEYS POLO CLUB
Carver Barracks, Saffron Walden, Essex

TAUNTON VALE POLO CLUB
Orchard Portmand, near Taunton

TIDWORTH POLO CLUB
Tidworth, Hants

TOULSTON POLO CLUB
Tadcaster, Yorkshire

WHITFIELD COURT POLO CLUB
Waterford, Ireland

Australian Polo Council

NEW SOUTH WALES
Affiliated Clubs: Goulburn, Tamarang, Toompang, County Gunnedah, Wirragulla, Quirindi, Muswelbrook, Forbes, Tally-Ho, Narromine, Wellington, Scone, Moree, Willow Tree, Vychan, Canberra, Tamworth, Warrun Bungle, Windsor, Rylstore

QUEENSLAND
Affiliated Clubs: Downs, Goondiwindi, Bulloo, Cannamulla

SOUTH AUSTRALIA
Affiliated Clubs: Adelaide, Mount Crawford, Strathalbyn, Broken Hill

VICTORIA
Affiliated Clubs: Hexham, Yarra Glen/Lilydale, Melbourne, Melbourne Hunt (Cranbourne)

WESTERN AUSTRALIA
Teams: Perth, Kojonup, Serpentine, Walkaway, Capel, Condingup

Barbados Polo Club

Holders, St James, Barbados, West Indies

Royal Brunei Polo Association

Affiliated Clubs: Jerudong Park, Berakas

Ghana Polo Association

Mile Six, Dodowa Road, Accra

Hong Kong Polo Association

Hong Kong

Indian Polo Association

CALCUTTA POLO CLUB
Calcutta

DELHI POLO CLUB
New Delhi

RAJASTHAN POLO CLUB
Rajasthan

REMOUNT AND VETERINARY CORPS POLO CLUB
Meerut-Cantt

AMATEUR RIDER CLUB
Bombay

DEHRA DUN POLO CLUB
Dehra Dun

INDIAN POLO ASSOCIATION
New Delhi

MADRAS POLO AND RIDERS' CLUB
Madras

POONA POLO CLUB
Poona

Royal Jordan Polo Club

Amman, Jordan

Kenya Polo Association

Affiliated Clubs: Manyatta (Gilgil), Nairobi, Nanyuki, North Kenya

Malayan Polo Association (1978)

Affiliated Clubs: Iskander, Penang, Royal Pahang, Royal Johore, Selangor, Trengganu

Malta Polo Club

Marsa Sports Ground

New Zealand Polo Association

AUCKLAND
Affiliated Clubs: Auckland, Cambridge, Glen Murray, Kihikihi, Lanherne, Morrinsville, Tangiteroria, Taupiri, Waimai

CENTRAL DISTRICTS
Affiliated Clubs: Hawkes Bay, Poverty Bay, Rangitikei, Wanstead

SOUTH ISLAND
Affiliated Clubs: Amuri, Ashburton, Ashley, Blenheim, Geraldine, Taieri

Nigerian Polo Association

Affiliated Clubs: Lagos, Ibadan, Kano, Katsina, Maidiguri, Jos, Port Harcourt, Sokoto, Kaduna, Accra Zaria

Royal Oman Polo Club

Oman

Pakistan Polo Association

Affiliated Clubs: Abbottabad, Chitral, Gilgit, Karachi, Kharian, Lahore, Multan, Nowshera, Peshawar, Rawalpindi, Baluchistan, Pakistan Railway, Punjab Police, Mona, ASC Club

Singapore Polo Club

Thomson Road, Singapore 1129

South African Polo Association

TRANSVAAL
Affiliated Clubs: East Rand, Inanda, New Scotland

NATAL
Affiliated Clubs: Bergville, Durban Shongweni, Gingindhlovu, Hillcrest, Karkloof, Kwambonambi, Lions River, Mooi River, Noodsberg, Ottawa, Ottos Bluff, Richmond, Stoney Hill

EAST GRIQUALAND
Affiliated Clubs: Kokstad, Matatiele, Swartberg, Lufafa Road, Underberg

ORANGE FREE STATE AND CAPE
Affiliated Clubs: Addo, Bloemfontein, Cape Hunt, Ficksburg, Harrismith, Rakhoi, Slabberts, Hammonia, Ladybrand, Senekai

United States Polo Association

N.B. There are upwards of 125 polo clubs in the United States. The following is a list of the more important clubs.

BRANDYWINE POLO CLUB
Toughkenamon, Pennsylvania

BROAD ACRES POLO CLUB
Norman, Oklahoma

CAMDEN POLO CLUB
Camden, South Carolina

CHUKKER VALLEY POLO CLUB
Gilbertsville, Pennsylvania

CINCINNATI POLO CLUB
Mason, Ohio

CLEVELAND POLO CLUB
Solon, Ohio

COLUMBUS POLO CLUB
Columbus, Ohio

DARLINGTON POLO CLUB
Darlington, Pennsylvania

DAYTON POLO CLUB
Dayton, Ohio

DULUTH POLO CLUB
Duluth, Minnesota

EAST AURORA POLO CLUB
East Aurora, New York

ELDORADO POLO CLUB
Palm Desert, California

FAIRFIELD POLO ASSOCIATION
Wichita, Kansas

FAIRLANE FARMS AT WELLINGTON
West Palm Beach, Florida

FARMINGTON HUNT CLUB
Charlottesville, Virginia

GREATER GRAND RAPIDS POLO CLUB
Grand Rapids, Michigan

HOUSTON POLO CLUB
Houston, Texas

JACKSON HOLE POLO CLUB
Jackson, Wyoming

JOY FARM POLO CLUB
Milwaukee, Wisconsin

KENTREE POLO CLUB
Grand Rapids, Michigan

LONGWOOD POLO CLUB
Carmel, Indiana

MAHONING VALLEY POLO CLUB
Canfield, Ohio